In Search of the Acadia
A Civil War Blockade Runner

British Built-Steam Powered River-Clyde Side Wheeler
American Civil War 1861-1865

By Eileen M. Benitz Wagner

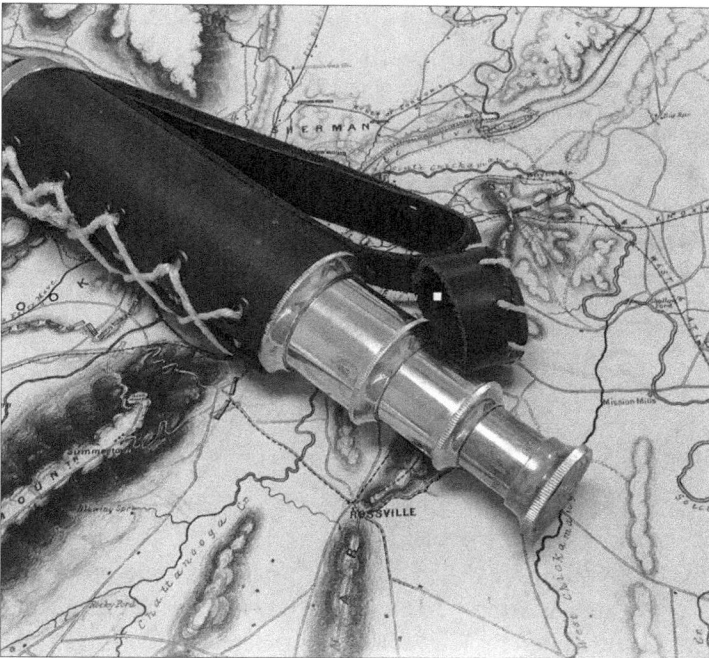

NorTex Press
An Imprint of Wild Horse Media Group
Fort Worth, Texas
www.WildHorseMedia.com

Based on the information I gathered during my research,
to the best of my knowledge, I believe this book to be accurate.

NorTex
★ **Press**

Copyright © 2019
By Eileen M. Benitz Wagner
Published By NorTex Press
An Imprint of Wild Horse Media Group
P.O. Box 331779
Fort Worth, Texas 76163
1-817-344-7036
www.WildHorseMedia.com
ALL RIGHTS RESERVED
1 2 3 4 5 6 7 8 9
ISBN-10: 1-68179-149-8
ISBN-13: 978-1-68179-149-4

Cover artwork is *Sinking of the "Acadia"* by Sherry Fullen Shelton and provided courtesy of the Brazoria County Historical Museum.

Dedication

Great care has been taken to this compilation and is dedicated to saving history of the Blockade Runner Acadia which ran aground during the American Civil War in Brazoria County, Texas.

Contents

Preface

A great deal has been written about the Canadian built Blockade Runner *Acadia*, it is my goal to compile as much as possible into one book.

Acknowledgements

Michael Bailey
Curator Brazoria County Historical Museum

John Choate
Diver/Instructor

Steve Stepinoff
Diver/Instructor

Mike Holt
Diver/Instructor

Andrew W. Hall
Galveston

Robby Roden
President, Sons of the Republic of Texas;
Stephen F. Austin Chapter #6

Ramon D. Torres
Edit

Introduction

The American Civil War 1861-1865. It is estimated the total number of ships to have been 1,650. Captured goods could bring 700 to 1,000 percent profit for the captain and crew of a Blockade Runner. This book is about the *Acadia*, a British built River-Clyde Side-wheel blockade-runner built in Sorel, Quebec, Canada. It was a state of the art design for her time.

She was very luxurious with accommodations for passengers.

Her captain, Thomas Leach, unfamiliar with the Texas coastline and in heavy fog, headed toward shore and ran her hard aground February 6, 1865, near San Luis Pass, Texas, where she remains today.

Much has been written about the *Acadia*. This book will try to compile as much as possible into one book. You will read several untold stories from divers that accompanied Dr. Wendell E. Pierce, D.D.S. and Archeologist, in the 1970 dives to retrieve artifacts from the sunken vessel.

Part One

British built steam-powered Side-Wheel River-Clyde design. Built for a mail carrier and luxury passenger ship in Sorel, Quebec, Canada in 1864. After a financial disastrous trip up the St. Lawrence River, because of her low design, she was coppered and converted to a Blockade Runner to service the Confederacy during the American Civil War.

Acadia flew under the British Maritime flag of the "Red Ensign," used by civilian vessels from Canada.[1]

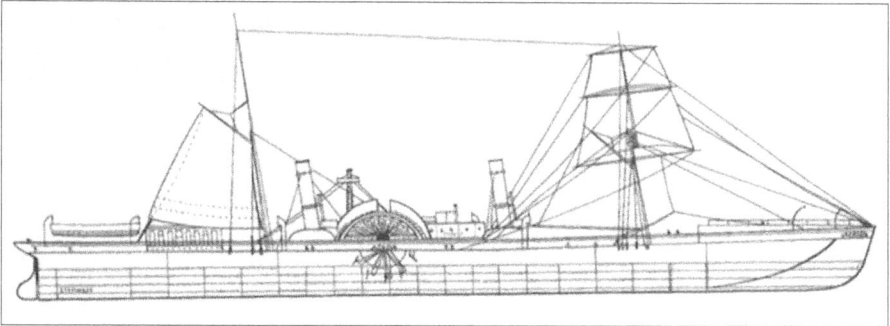

British Built River Clyde—Steam Powered with a Paddlewheel. *Drawing courtesy John Choate, artist Steve Stepinoff.*

"ACADIA"
The American Civil War

The Paris Agreement of 1856 described a blockade as an instrument of war, only to be used between separate nations for the purpose of conquest. The treaty of Paris stated, " A Blockade to be effective must be complete."

I hereby authorize and direct the Secretary of State to affix the Seal of the United States to a Proclamation letting (setting?) on foot a Blockade of the ports of the states of South Carolina, Georgia, Alabama, Florida, Mississippi, Louisiana and Texas.

Dated this day and signed by me and for so doing this shall be his warrant.

Abraham Lincoln

Washington, 19th April 1861[2]

1

Under Mr. Lincoln's orders, a blockade was declared from the Virginia Capes to the Rio Grande River in Texas. This proclamation of blockade of "all Southern Ports" came before a number for the Southern states had ever seceded from the Union. States now involved hastened to secede and large numbers of officers in the United States Army and Navy resigned their commissions to offer services to their home states.

President Abraham Lincoln[3]

The United States could not blockade itself, therefore, President Lincoln declared the "South" a separate nation.

At the beginning of the war, the Federal Navy was ineffective. However, the Confederate Navy was worse, and the Confederacy did not have the industrial capability to build ships of war. Accelerated production put ships afloat for the Federal Navy at a rate never witnessed before in the United State Naval history, thereby increasing the effect of the blockade. The Confederate Navy was extremely small, and merchant and ship-owners supported a privateering policy proclaimed by President Jefferson Davis two days before President Lincoln announced the Federal Blockade.

Civil War Blockade Shipyard

Foreign governments got involved with building and running the blockade ships for huge profits. Two such building sites were Clyde River Shipyards, Gourock, Scotland and Sorel, Quebec, Canada.

During the Civil War, Canada favored the Confederacy and had been doing export and import business with the South. The Nova Scotia ports of Saint John and Halifax became one of the

President Jefferson Davis

most heavily defended harbors in the British Empire. Fortunes made with just one successful trip. Sorel, Quebec began building Clyde side-wheel steamers to fill the orders for new vessels that Scotland could not manufacture.

Scotland's Role in the American Civil War

Their Clyde-built steamers played a huge role in breaking through the Union's blockades to deliver goods and food to the South. The South needed arms and a way to ship cotton etc., to Europe, thus adding foreign currency to their economy. It was a gamble for the Captain and crew but the rewards were high. Even two successful trips could pay for the building of a blockade-runner. It was all profit after that.

In 1864 twenty-seven Clyde side-wheel shipyards employed 25,000 men. Fifty blockade-runners were completed and launched in that year. 3,000 Scots served on these vessels. The need for greater efficiency and faster speed led John Elder to design and develop the compound engine.[4]

The Blockade Proclamation

The blockade proclamation was unique since the Federal Government could not enforce such a blockade. At that time the United States had less than a hundred-fifty vessels, and only forty vessels had crews. The rest were out of commission.

The British Government regarded President Lincoln's proclamation as a paper blockade because it could not be enforced. The Federal Government insisted that a state of war did not exist, but only in insurrection and that no other country had the right to intervene. Britain, France, Spain, the Netherlands, and Brazil saw the situation differently as shown by their declaration of neutrality. This declaration recognized that the Confederate States were a separate power and that Confederate ships, would have the same privileges in neutral ports United States ships. Another law of the blockade was that a vessel was not proscribed unless it was bound for a blockaded port and could not be interfered with until that time. The establishment of bases on foreign territory close to the Confederacy meant that ships could enter these ports in complete security. Two days before, President Jefferson Davis announced a privateering policy.

Senator Charles Sumner of Massachusetts holding the blockade proclamation a mistake said that Lincoln proclaimed a closing of the rebel ports, instead of a blockade; there could concession of belligerency. The whole case of England is made to stand on the use of the word "blockade. *The Paris Treaty of 1856* described a blockade as an instrument of war, only to be used between separate nations for the purpose of conquest. The Treaty of Paris also stated, "A Blockade to be effective must be complete."

Privateering was internationally outlawed, but President Davis was repeating what the United States had done in the Revolution and the War of 1812, in supplying the Navy by private armed vessels flying the Confederate flag. Lincoln proclaimed privateering as piracy and punishable by death but rescinded this severe penalty by another proclamation March 1863. The strengthened blockade forces caused a scarcity of critical items in the South after the fall of New Orleans in 1862, making it essential to increase the import trade. Blockade running then became big business and more profitable than privateering. It was also patriotic.

Had the South taken advantage of the weak blockading efforts during its first year no doubt counter-balance would have resulted. Ironically, Federal Navy weakness of 1861 created southern apathy towards the blockade thereby allowing strangulation of vital imports by the latter progressively strengthening blockade.

The later blockade results were first realized in the south by private enterprises, which commenced to import goods in vast quantities for their own survival. Had the Confederate Government reached with the same foresight and utilized the opportunity to import critical war material and make proper negotiations with foreign nations, its own emasculation might not have occurred.

The privateer who transformed the blockade running found it to be a well-organized, sound and efficient business completely British administered using British seamen and British ships. Due to the influence of her consort, Prince Albert, Queen Victoria issued a royal proclamation of strict British neutrality and that the federal blockade would be respected. However, Britons were in the middle of the blockade running business. Most of the vessels were built in Mersey or Clyde shipyards. Had it not been for Prince Albert, England may have allied with the Confederacy against the United States.

With the rules set by international law and respected by the Federal Government, the blockade-running strategy was clearly established. So the ball game started. Neutral ports such as Halifax, Nassau, Bermuda, Havana, Vera Cruz, and Matamoros were used as bases. Cargos were shipped to these bases from Europe and the same ships returned to Europe with cargos, primarily cotton, delivered to these ports by Confederate blockade runners.

Nassau, in the Bahamas, was five hundred sixty miles from Charleston and six hundred miles from Wilmington but was neutral territory even though the Bahamas extended to within fifty miles of the American coast. This close proximity quickly established Nassau as the main base for blockade-runners and most important single way station on the sea road to the Confederacy became, for a brief time, the time where fortunes could be made more quickly than anywhere else on earth. The harbor was full of ships, the wharves were piled with freight and the streets, inns and drinking places were crowded with men who had much money to spend and not much time to spend it and who knew that no matter how much they spent they would get it all back in a very few days.

Nassau, in short, was the center of a hell-raising boom. No merchant ever imagined anything like the profits that were made there. Freight charges on Confederate imports ran fifty pounds sterling per ton, even to one hundred pounds, and a cargo of five hundred bales of cotton could earn fifty pounds or more for each bale. It was common knowledge that one successful trip even though the blockade was sufficient to repay owners the full purchase price of the vessel, and many grew rich.

Southern demand for munitions, arms, medicine, foodstuff, and luxury items was high, as was world demand for Confederate exports, such as cotton and naval stores (turpentine, pitch, and tar increased in value by 1000% during the war). Despite initial uncertainties and restrictions, the Civil War brought prosperity to most sectors of the Maritimes' economy. Exports from Nova Scotia to the US, including fish and coal, doubled in value from 1861 to war's end. Fishermen, farmers, miners, lumbermen, and mercantile benefitted. New Brunswick's timber and shipbuilding industries continued to expand.

Sailors received the unheard of wage of $100.00 a round trip through the blockade plus $50.00 bonus. A ship's captain could earn $5,000.00 for a round trip and in addition, he could carry a certain amount of freight on his own account. Passenger rates were naturally high, varying from $300.00 to $500.00 essential supplies commanded exceptionally high prices as much as $2,500.00 for a small box of medicine. This makes for World War II and subsequent black market prices look like a bargain basement fire sale during the depression.

Many of the vessels running the blockade were side-wheelers, paddle-steamers of the 400 to 600 tons burden and with a caring capacity of anything 600 to 1,000 cotton bales of 500 pounds each. As cotton could be bought for eight cents a pound in Wilmington and sold for fifty cents a pound in Liverpool, and huge profits were made. It was common for the outward trip to show a profit of $100,000.00 and for the return trip to show a profit of $125,000.00. In the first year of the blockade, profits of 100 to 200% were common. Later they rose to 2,000%. During most of the first year of the war, cautious British shippers refused to run the blockade with anything but their oldest, least valuable vessels. Nevertheless, 800 vessels entered and cleared from Confederate ports and less than 10% of these runners were caught. Again, I must say that the blockade-runners failed to make the most of the best opportunities of the war. By 1865, the blockading fleet at Charleston and Wilmington alone were more than 150 vessels. This was greater than the whole Federal Navy at the start of the war.

After the first year of the war, it became more difficult to break the blockade; it was necessary to obtain speedy, efficient vessels for this purpose. The River Clyde Steamers was ideally suited in every way for the block-running business. From about 1862 onward, ships were sought but the purchasers preferred to remain unknown, using fictitious names.

Names of vessels were changed frequently making it difficult to determine which vessels were active blockade-runners. However, it was well known that the River Clyde Steamers proved the most successful vessels in the entire blockade-running trade and fared as friends of the South.

Using the River Clyde Steamer style of marine architecture, two Canadian businessmen decided to build the "Utopian" of all blockade-runners in the spring of 1864. The businessmen were: Jacques Felix Sincennes(sic)[6] of Sorel, Province of Canada and William McNaughton of Montreal. The ship was to be the most elegant, strongest, fastest, and able to carry more cargo than any of her sister blockade-runners. Her name was to be the ACADIA. The construction site was the shipyards of Sorel, Province of Canada. The choicest of Canadian timbers were hewn for the frame. The design was perfected to the millimeter. Custom made fittings of heavy lead

SCOTT'S GREAT SNAKE.
Cartoon map illustrating Gen. Winfield Scott's plan to crush the Confederacy, economically. It is sometimes called the "ANACONDA PLAN."
The Library of Congress
Published by J.B. Elliott, Cincinnati, 1861

The Confederate States of the American Civil War.

and brass pipes with brass pin cut-off valves were all of the highest quality. The entire bottom of brass sheeting secured with brass nails. The boilers and machinery were examples of precision engineering. She was as sound and sturdy as the Canadian dollar and built to last an eternity. Her register tonnage was 738.45. Her sister ships were usually 400 to 600 tons burden. The *ACADIA* had one engine of 900 horsepower to push her paddle wheels, twice the horsepower of most other blockade-runners. The engine room alone was 81 feet long. The overall length was 211 feet 11 inches.

On May 10, 1864, construction started and was completed on July 14, 1864. She had schooner rigging with two masts, round stern and was Caravel built. The registry date was October 31, 1864, at one o'clock, at Montreal. The two proud owners were now ready to choose a Captain and so did in Captain Thomas Leach of Halifax and they empowered him to sell the ship with no minimum price named, at any place out of the Province of Canada within 12 months from the date of certificate, which was the same as the registry date, October 31, 1864.[7]

Funding the Civil War with an Income Tax

President Lincoln on August 5, 1862, signed the congressional bill to institute the nations' first income tax to help pay for the Civil war. Thus paving the way for the modern tax code.

Nevada's contribution to the war was the Comstock Lode, a silver mine totaling $400 million in value helped finance the Union war effort to defeat the southern states.[8]

The Confederacy relied mostly on cotton and tobacco imports, exports, and tariffs. A "war-tax" was enacted but it was difficult to collect.

Civil War Timeline

November 6, 1860 - Abraham Lincoln is elected sixteenth president of the United States, the first Republican president in the nation who represents a party that opposes the spread of slavery in the territories of the United States.
December 17, 1860 - The first Secession Convention meets in Columbia, South Carolina.
December 20, 1860 - South Carolina secedes from the Union.
January 1861 - Six additional southern states secede from the

Union.

February 8-9, 1861 - The southern states that seceded create a government at Montgomery, Alabama, and the Confederate States of America are formed.

February 18, 1861 - Jefferson Davis is appointed the first President of the Confederate States of America at Montgomery, Alabama, a position he will hold until elections can be arranged.

March 4, 1861 - Abraham Lincoln is inaugurated as the sixteenth president of the United States in Washington, DC.

April 12, 1861 - Southern forces fire upon Fort Sumter, South Carolina. The Civil War has formally begun.

April 15, 1861 - President Lincoln issues a public declaration that an insurrection exists and calls for 75,000 militia to stop the rebellion. As a result of this call for volunteers, four additional southern states secede from the Union in the following weeks. Lincoln will respond on May 3 with an additional call for 43,000+ volunteers to serve for three years, expanding the size of the Regular Army.

April 19, 1861 - Federal Blockade by President Lincoln

May 24, 1861 - Union forces cross the Potomac River and occupy Arlington Heights, the home of future Confederate General Robert E. Lee. It is during the occupation of nearby Alexandria that Colonel Elmer Ellsworth, commander of the 11th New York Infantry and a close friend of the Lincolns, is shot dead by the owner of the Marshall House just after removing a Confederate flag from its roof.

June 3, 1861 - A skirmish near Philippi in western Virginia, is the first clash of Union and Confederate forces in the east.

June 10, 1861- Battle of Big Bethel, the first land battle of the war in Virginia.

June 20, 1861 - At the culmination of the Wheeling Convention, the region that composed the northwestern counties of Virginia broke away from that state to form West Virginia, officially designated and accepted as the thirty-fifth state of the Union on June 20, 1863.

July 21, 1861 - The Battle of Bull Run (or First Manassas), is fought near Manassas, Virginia. The Union Army under General Irwin McDowell initially succeeds in driving back Confederate forces under General Pierre Gustav Toutant Beauregard, but the arrival of troops under General Joseph E. Johnston initiates a series of reverses that sends McDowell's army in a panicked retreat to the defenses of Washington. It is here that Thomas Jonathan Jackson, a professor at VMI, will receive everlasting fame as "Stonewall" Jackson.

July 1861 - To thwart the Confederate threat in northern Virginia, a series of earthworks and forts are engineered to surround the City of Washington, adding to protection already offered by active posts such as Fort Washington on the Potomac River.

August 10, 1861 - Battle of Wilson's Creek, Missouri. The Union Army under General Nathaniel Lyon, attack Confederate troops and state militia southwest of Springfield, Missouri, and after a disastrous day that included the death of Lyon, are thrown back. The Confederate victory emphasizes the strong southern presence west of the Mississippi River.

August 28-29, 1861 - Fort Hatteras at Cape Hatteras, North Carolina, falls to Union naval forces. This begins the first Union efforts to close southern ports along the Carolina coast.

September 20, 1861 - Lexington, Missouri falls to Confederate forces under Sterling Price.

October 21, 1861 - Battle of Ball's Bluff, Virginia. Colonel Edward D. Baker, senator from Oregon and a friend of President Lincoln, led troops across the Potomac River only to be forced back to the river's edge where he was killed. The ensuing Union withdrawal turned into a rout with many soldiers drowning while trying to re-cross the icy waters of the Potomac River.

January 19, 1862 - Battle of Mill Springs, Kentucky. The Union victory weakened the Confederate hold on the state.

February 6, 1862 - Surrender of Fort Henry, Tennessee. The loss of this southern fort on the Tennessee River opened the door to Union control of the river.

February 8, 1862 - Battle of Roanoke Island, North Carolina. A Confederate defeat, the battle resulted in Union occupation of eastern North Carolina and control of Pamlico Sound, to be used as Northern base for further operations against the southern coast.

February 16, 1862 - Surrender of Fort Donelson, Tennessee. This primary southern fort on the Cumberland River left the river in Union hands. It was here that Union General Ulysses S. Grant gained his nickname "Unconditional Surrender".

February 22, 1862 - Jefferson Davis is inaugurated as President of the Confederate States of America.

March 7-8, 1862 - Battle of Pea Ridge (Elkhorn Tavern), Arkansas. The Union victory loosened the Confederate hold on Missouri and disrupted southern control of a portion of the

Mississippi River.

March 9, 1862 - The naval battle between the USS *Monitor* and the *CSS Virginia* (the old USS *Merrimack*), the first "ironclads", is fought in Hampton Roads, Virginia.

April 6-7, 1862 - The Battle of Shiloh (Pittsburg Landing), the first major battle in Tennessee. Confederate General Albert Sidney Johnston, a veteran of the Texas War of Independence and the War with Mexico considered to be one of the finest officers the South has, is killed on the first day of fighting. The Union victory further secures the career of Union General Ulysses S. Grant.

April 24-25, 1862 - A Union fleet of gunships under Admiral David Farragut passes Confederate forts guarding the mouth of the Mississippi River. On April 25, the fleet arrived at New Orleans where they demanded the surrender of the city. Within two days the forts fall into Union hands and the mouth of the great river is under Union control.

May 25, 1862 - First Battle of Winchester, Virginia. After two weeks of maneuvering and battles at Cross Keys and Front Royal, General "Stonewall" Jackson attacks Union forces at Winchester and successfully drives them from the city. The victory is the culmination of his 1862 Valley Campaign.

May 31-June 1, 1862 - The Battle of Seven Pines near Richmond, Virginia. General Joseph Johnston, commander of the Confederate army in Virginia is wounded and replaced by Robert E. Lee who renames his command the "Army of Northern Virginia.

June 6, 1862 - Battle of Memphis, Tennessee. A Union flotilla under Commodore Charles Davis successfully defeats a Confederate river force on the Mississippi River near the city and Memphis surrenders. The Mississippi River is now in Union control except for its course west of Mississippi where the city of Vicksburg stands as the last southern stronghold on the great river.

June 25-July 1, 1862 - The Seven Days' Battles before Richmond. General Lee's army attacks the "Army of the Potomac" under General George McClellan in a succession of battles beginning at Mechanicsville on June 26 and ending at Malvern Hill on July 1.

August 30-31, 1862 - The Battle of Second Bull Run (or Second Manassas) is fought on the same ground where one year before, the Union army was defeated and sent reeling in retreat to Washington. Likewise, the result of this battle is a Union defeat.

September 17, 1862 - The Battle of Antietam (or Sharpsburg), Maryland, the bloodiest single day of the Civil War. The result of the battle ends General Lee's first invasion of the North. Following the Union victory, President Lincoln will introduce the *Emancipation Proclamation*, an executive order that freed every slave in the Confederate States.

December 13, 1862 - The Battle of Fredericksburg, Virginia. The Army of the Potomac, under General Ambrose Burnside, is soundly defeated by Lee's forces after a risky river crossing and sacking of the city.

December 31-January 3, 1863 - Battle of Stones River, Tennessee. Fought between the Union Army of the Cumberland under General William Rosecrans and the Confederate Army of Tennessee under General Braxton Bragg, the costly Union victory frees middle Tennessee from Confederate control and boosts northern morale.

January 1, 1863 - The *Emancipation Proclamation* goes into effect. Applauded by many abolitionists including Frederick Douglass, there are others who feel it does not go far enough to totally abolish slavery.

March 3, 1863 - Conscription, or the drafting of soldiers into military service, begins in the North. It had begun in the South the year before.

April 1863 - Union forces in the east begin a new campaign in Virginia to flank Lee's Army of Northern Virginia at Fredericksburg. In the west, a Union army has begun a campaign to surround and take Vicksburg, Mississippi, the last Confederate stronghold on the Mississippi River.

May 1-4, 1863 - The Battle of Chancellorsville, Virginia. General Lee's greatest victory is marred by the mortal wounding of "Stonewall" Jackson, who dies on May 10. Soon after, Lee asks Jefferson Davis for permission to invade the North and take the war out of Virginia.

May 18, 1863 - Siege of Vicksburg, Mississippi begins. Union forces under General Ulysses S. Grant attack Confederate defenses outside the city on May 19-22. If Vicksburg falls, the Mississippi River will be completely controlled by the Union.

June 9, 1863 - The Battle of Brandy Station, Virginia. Union cavalry forces cross the Rapidan River to attack General J.E.B. Stuart's cavalry and discover that Lee's men are moving west toward the Shenandoah Valley. The largest cavalry battle of the Civil War, it also marks the beginning of the Gettysburg

Campaign. Meanwhile, the Union assault on Vicksburg, Mississippi has become a siege of the city where soldiers and civilians alike suffer from constant bombardment.

June 14-15, 1863 - Battle of Second Winchester, Virginia. Confederate troops under General Richard Ewell defeat Union troops under General Robert Milroy, clearing the Shenandoah Valley of Union forces.

June 28, 1863 - The Gettysburg Campaign continues. Confederates pass through York and reach the bridge over the Susquehanna River at Columbia, but Union militia set fire to the bridge, denying access to the east shore. Southern cavalry skirmishes with Union militia near Harrisburg, Pennsylvania.

July 1-3, 1963 - The Battle of Gettysburg, Pennsylvania. The bloodiest battle of the Civil War dashes Robert E. Lee's hopes for a successful invasion of the North.

July 4, 1963 - Vicksburg, Mississippi, surrenders to the Union Army under Grant. The capture of Vicksburg gives the Union complete control of the Mississippi River, a vital supply line for the Confederate states in the west. At Gettysburg, Lee begins his retreat to Virginia.

July 10-11, 1863 - Union naval and land forces attack confederate defenses near Charleston, South Carolina. Among the Union troops is the 54th Massachusetts Colored Infantry, the first African American regiment of volunteers to see combat.

July 13, 1863 - Draft Riots begin in New York City and elsewhere as disgruntled workers and laborers, seething over the draft system that seemingly favors the rich, attack the draft office and African American churches. The riots continue through July 16.

July 13-14, 1863 - Near Falling Waters, Maryland, Union troops skirmish with Lee's rearguard. That night the Army of Northern Virginia crosses the Potomac River and the Gettysburg Campaign ends.

July 18, 1863 - Second Assault on Battery Wagner, South Carolina. Leading the Union infantry charge is the 54th Massachusetts Colored Infantry commanded by Colonel Robert Gould Shaw who is killed and buried with the dead of his regiment.

August 21, 1863 - Sacking of Lawrence, Kansas. In a murderous daylight raid, Confederate and Missouri guerillas under William Clarke Quantrill storm into Lawrence and destroy most of the town. Approximately 150 men and boys are murdered by Quantrill's men.

September 9, 1863 - Chattanooga, Tennessee, is occupied by

Union forces under General William Rosecrans whose Army of the Cumberland will soon invade northern Georgia.

September 19-20, 1863 - The Battle of Chickamauga, Georgia. The Union Army of the Cumberland under General William Rosecrans is defeated and nearly routed by the Confederate Army of Tennessee commanded by General Braxton Bragg. Rosecrans' army retreats to the supply base at Chattanooga, Tennessee.

September –November 1863 - The Siege of Chattanooga, Tennessee. Confederate forces under Braxton Bragg surround the occupied city. General Ulysses S. Grant is assigned to command the troops there and begins immediate plans to relieve the besieged Union army.

October 5, 1863 - Outside of Charleston Harbor, the Confederate *David*, a partially submerged, steam-powered vessel, attacked the *New Ironsides*, part of the Union fleet blockading the harbor, with a torpedo. Both ships survived the attack, though the commander of the *David* and one of his crew were captured.

October 9 - 22, 1863 - Bristoe Station Campaign. In a feint toward Washington, Lee's Army of the Northern Virginia marches into northern Virginia in an attempt to flank the Army of the Potomac, under General Meade. Lee successfully outmaneuvers Meade though fails to bring him to battle or catch him in the open. An engagement at Bristoe Station, Virginia, on October 14 gives the campaign its name.

November 19, 1863 - Dedication of the Soldiers' National Cemetery at Gettysburg. President Abraham Lincoln delivers the *Gettysburg Address*.

November 23-25, 1863 - The Battle for Chattanooga. Union forces break the Confederate siege of the city in successive attacks. The most notable event is the storming of Lookout Mountain on November 24 and the Battle of Missionary Ridge the following day. The decisive Union victory sends the Confederate Army south into Georgia where General Bragg reorganizes his forces before resigning from command on November 30.

November 26-December 1, 1863 - The Mine Run Campaign. Meade's Army of the Potomac marches against Lee's Army of Northern Virginia south of the Rapidan River, east of Orange Court House. Lee reacts and throws up a line of defenses along the banks of Mine Run Creek. After several days of probing the defenses, Meade withdraws north of the Rapidan and goes into winter quarters.

November 27 to December 3, 1863 - Siege of Knoxville, Tennessee. Confederate troops under General James Longstreet lay siege to the city of Knoxville held by Union forces under General Ambrose Burnside. Longstreet finally attacks on November 30 but is repulsed with heavy losses. The arrival of Union reinforcements forces him to withdraw to Greeneville, Tennessee, where his corps will spend the winter.

December 8, 1863 - Lincoln Issues his *Proclamation of Amnesty and Reconstruction*, which would pardon those who participated in the "existing rebellion" if they take an oath to the Union.

February 9, 1864 - Escape from Libby Prison, Richmond. After weeks of digging, 109 Union officers made their escape from the notorious Libby Prison, the largest and most sensational escape of the war. Though 48 of the escapees were later captured and two drowned, 59 were able to make their way into Union lines.

February 27, 1864 - In Georgia, Camp Sumter Prison Camp opens. Universally referred to as Andersonville Prison Camp, it will become notorious for overcrowded conditions and a high death rate among its inmates.

February 14-20, 1864 - Union Capture and Occupation of Meridian, Mississippi. Union forces under William T. Sherman enter the city of Meridian, Mississippi after a successful month of campaigning through the central part of the state. The capture of this important southern town, well known for its industry and storage capabilities, severely hampers the efforts of Confederate commanders to sustain their armies in the deep south, Georgia and west of the Mississippi River.

February 17, 1864 - First Successful Submarine Attack of the Civil War. The CSS *H.L. Hunley,* a seven-man submergible craft, attacked the USS *Houstonic* outside of Charleston, South Carolina. Struck by the submarine's torpedo, the *Housatonic* broke apart and sank, taking all but five of her crew with her. Likewise, the *Hunley* was also lost and never heard from again until discovered in 1995 at the spot where it sank after the attack.

March 2, 1864 - Ulysses S. Grant is appointed lieutenant general, a rank revived at the request of President Lincoln. Grant assumes command of all Union Armies in the field the following day.

March 10, 1864 - The Red River Campaign begins. As part of an overall Union strategy to strike deep into various parts of the Confederacy, a combined force of army and navy commands under General Nathaniel Banks begins a campaign on the Red River in Louisiana.

April 8, 1864 - Battle of Sabine Crossroads or Mansfield, Louisiana, the first major battle of the Red River Campaign in Louisiana.

April 9, 1864 - Battle of Pleasant Hill, Louisiana. The Union Army under Banks defeats the attempt by Confederate forces under General Richard Taylor to drive them out of Louisiana. Unfortunately, the result of the campaign would be less than desired as it drew to a close in the first week of May with Confederates still in firm control of most of the state.

April 12, 1864 - Capture of Fort Pillow, Tennessee. After a rapid raid through central and western Tennessee, Confederate cavalry under Nathan Bedford Forrest attacked and overwhelmed the Union garrison at Fort Pillow, located on the Mississippi River. Among those garrisoning the fort were African American troops, many of whom were murdered by Forrest's angered troopers after they had surrendered. The affair was investigated and though charges of an atrocity were denied by Confederate authorities, the events at Fort Pillow cast a pall over Forrest's reputation and remained an emotional issue throughout the remainder of the war and after.

May 4-5, 1864 - Battle of the Wilderness, Virginia, the opening battle of the "Overland Campaign" or "Wilderness Campaign". General Ulysses S. Grant, accompanying the Army of the Potomac under General Meade, issued orders for the campaign to begin on May 3. Lee responded by attacking the Union column in the dense woods and underbrush of an area known as the Wilderness, west of Fredericksburg, Virginia.

May 7, 1864 - Beginning of the Atlanta Campaign. With three Union armies under his command, General William T. Sherman marched south from Tennessee into Georgia against the Confederate Army of Tennessee under General Joseph Johnston, the objective being the city of Atlanta.

May 8-21, 1864 - Battle of Spotsylvania Court House, Virginia. Lee successfully stalls Grant's drive toward Richmond.

May 11, 1864 - Battle of Yellow Tavern. Six miles north of Richmond, Confederate cavalry under General J.E.B. Stuart blocked a force of Union cavalry under General Philip Sheridan. General Stuart was mortally wounded during the encounter.

May 14-15, 1864 - Battle of Resaca, Georgia. General Sherman's armies are blocked at Resaca by General Johnston's Army of Tennessee. After two days of maneuvering and intense fighting, Johnston withdraws. Sherman will advance but take precautions against ordering any further massed assaults where high casualties may occur.

June 1-3, 1864 - Battle of Cold Harbor, Virginia. Relentless and bloody Union attacks fail to dislodge Lee's army from its strong line of defensive works northeast of Richmond.

June 8, 1864 - Abraham Lincoln is nominated by his party for a second term as president.

June 10, 1864 - Battle of Brice's Crossroads, Mississippi- In spite of being outnumbered almost two to one, Confederate General Nathan Bedford Forrest attacks and routs the Union command under General Samuel Sturgis.

June 15-18, 1864 - Assault on Petersburg, Virginia. After withdrawing from the lines at Cold Harbor, the Army of the Potomac crossed the James River and with troops from the Army of the James attacked the outer defenses of Petersburg, the primary junction for several southern railroads. After four days of bloody attacks, Grant accepts that only a siege can systematically isolate the city and cut off Confederate supplies to the capital of Richmond.

June 19, 1864 - The USS *Kearsarge* sinks the Confederate raider CSS *Alabama* near Cherbourg, France.

June 27, 1864 - Battle of Kennesaw Mountain, Georgia. After weeks of maneuvering and battles, Sherman's Army of the Cumberland and Army of the Tennessee smash headlong into Johnston's carefully planned defenses at Big and Little Kennesaw. Johnston remains on this line until July 2, when he retreats at the threat being flanked by Sherman's mobile force.

July 9, 1864 - Battle of Monocacy, Maryland. In an attempt to draw Union troops away from the ongoing siege of Petersburg and Richmond, a Confederate force under Jubal Early quietly moved north into Maryland. Early had made excellent progress until he reached Frederick, Maryland, where a force of 6,000 Federal troops under General Lew Wallace, was arrayed to delay his advance. Though the battle was a Union defeat, it was also touted as "the battle that saved Washington" for it succeeded in holding back Early's march until troops could be sent to the capital's defense.

July 11-12, 1864 - Attack on the Defenses of Washington. Jubal Early's troops arrive on the outskirts of Washington, D.C, and trade cannon fire with a token Union force remaining in the forts around the city. President Lincoln observes the skirmishing from Fort Stevens as reinforcements from the Army of the Potomac arrive and quickly fill in the works. Early withdraws that evening.

July 14-15, 1864 - Battles near Tupelo, Mississippi. The Union defeat of Nathan Bedford Forrest secured the supply lines to Sherman's armies operating against Atlanta, Georgia.

July 17, 1864 - General John Bell Hood replaces General Joseph Johnston as commander of the Army of Tennessee. This change in command signals a new Confederate strategy to thwart Sherman's campaign, though the end result will be disastrous for the southern cause.

July 20, 1864 - Battle of Peachtree Creek, Georgia, the first major battle around the city of Atlanta. General Hood sends his army out of the city's defenses to attack the approaching Federal troops under George Thomas. After several hours of fierce fighting, Hood withdrew back to his own defensive works.

July 21, 1864 - The Battle of Atlanta. Hood's second effort to throw back Union forces under Sherman brings him heavy casualties with no positive results. General James McPherson, commander of the Union Army of the Tennessee, is killed during the fighting.

July 30, 1864 - The Battle of the Crater at Petersburg, Virginia. After a month of tunneling by soldiers of the 48th Pennsylvania Infantry, a massive mine was exploded under a Confederate fort in the Petersburg siege lines. The infantry charge that followed was poorly coordinated and by day's end, confederate counterattacks had driven out the Union troops and the siege lines remained unchanged.

August 5, 1864 - Battle of Mobile Bay. A Union fleet under Admiral David Farragut steamed into Mobile Bay outside the city of Mobile, Alabama, defended by two strong forts and a small southern flotilla, including the formidable ironclad *CSS Tennessee*. Farragut's ships defeated the Confederate ships and bypassed the forts, capturing the important southern port.

August 18-19, 1864 - Battles on the Weldon Railroad near Petersburg, Virginia. Union attempts to capture this important railroad into Petersburg were stopped by Confederate counterattacks. Despite southern efforts, the Union remained in firm possession of their gains and the railroad.

August 25, 1864 - Battle of Ream's Station, near Petersburg,

Virginia. A surprise Confederate counterattack briefly stopped Union destruction of the Weldon Railroad near Ream's Station, though failed to release the Union grip on this important supply line into Petersburg.

August 31, - September 1, 1864 - Battle of Jonesborough, Georgia. The final southern counterattack against Union troops outside the city of Atlanta fails.

September 1, 1864 - Fall of Atlanta, Georgia. Confederate troops under General Hood evacuate the city of Atlanta. General Sherman's army occupies the city and its defenses the following day.

September 19, 1864 - Third Battle of Winchester, Virginia. Union forces under General Philip Sheridan attacked the Confederate army under Jubal Early near the city of Winchester and drove them southward, up the Shenandoah Valley.

September 22, 1864 - Battle of Fisher's Hill, Virginia. The Union Army of the Shenandoah under General Philip Sheridan attacked Jubal Early's Confederates near Fisher's Hill, overpowering the southerners and again forcing them to flee the battlefield. Union officers and officials in Washington believe this to be the final battle in the Shenandoah Valley.

September 29-30, 1864 - Battle of Fort Harrison near Richmond, Virginia. In a sweeping assault, the Confederate stronghold known as Fort Harrison falls to the Army of the James. Confederate efforts to retake the fort fail.

October 19, 1864 - The Battle of Cedar Creek, Virginia. In an early morning surprise attack, Jubal Early's Confederates successfully attack and drive troops of the Army of the Shenandoah from their camps on the banks of Cedar Creek south of Middletown, Virginia. Hearing the fight from his headquarters at Winchester, General Philip Sheridan rides southward, rallying dispirited troops who return to the battlefield. By day's end, Early's forces are put to flight. Despite several attempts to disrupt the Union advance in the coming weeks, the battle for control of the Shenandoah Valley is over.

November 8, 1864 - Abraham Lincoln is reelected president of the United States.

November 16, 1864 - General Sherman's Army of Georgia begins the "March to the Sea"

November 30, 1864 - Battle of Franklin, Tennessee. After a month of raiding Sherman's supply lines and attacking Union outposts, John Bell Hood's army confronts Union troops from General John Schofield's command, who they had encountered the day before near Spring Hill, Tennessee. A massive frontal assault on the well-entrenched Federal line meets with disaster. Despite some taking of outside works and defenses, the toll for Hood's forces is too heavy including the loss of six of his generals. Union troops retreat in the direction of Nashville.

December 10, 1864 - Harassed only by scattered Georgia militia, Sherman's Army of Georgia arrives at Savannah, Georgia, completing the famous "March to the Sea". At Savannah, his troops will take Fort McAllister and force Confederate defenders to evacuate the city.

December 15-16, 1864 - The Battle of Nashville, Tennessee. The Confederate Army under John Bell Hood is thoroughly defeated and the threat to Tennessee ends.

January 15, 1865 - Assault and capture of Fort Fisher, North Carolina. Union occupation of this fort at the mouth of the Cape Fear River closes access to Wilmington, the last southern seaport on the east coast that was open to blockade runners and commercial shipping.

February 1, 1865 - Sherman's Army leaves Savannah to march through the Carolinas.

February 17, 1865 - Sherman's Army captures Columbia, South Carolina while Confederate defenders evacuate Charleston, South Carolina.

February 22, 1865 - Wilmington, N.C., falls to Union troops, closing the last important southern port on the east coast. On this same day, Joseph E. Johnston is restored to command the nearly shattered Army of the Tennessee, vice John B. Hood who resigned a month earlier.

March 4, 1865 - President Abraham Lincoln is inaugurated for his second term as president in Washington, D.C.

March 11, 1865 - Sherman's Army occupies Fayetteville, North Carolina.

March 16 and 19-21, 1865 - The Battles of Averasborough and Bentonville, North Carolina. Sherman's army is stalled in its drive northward from Fayetteville but succeeds in passing around the Confederate forces toward its object of Raleigh.

March 25, 1865 - Attack on Fort Stedman, Petersburg, Virginia. Touted as "Lee's last offensive", Confederate troops under General John B. Gordon attack and briefly capture the Union fort in the Petersburg siege lines in an attempt to thwart Union plans for a late March assault. By day's end, the southerners have been thrown out and the lines remain unchanged.

April 1, 1865 - The Battle of Five Forks, Virginia. The Confederate defeat at Five Forks initiates General Lee's decision to abandon the Petersburg-Richmond siege lines.

April 2, 1865 - The Fall of Petersburg and Richmond. General Lee abandons both cities and moves his army west in hopes of joining Confederate forces under General Johnston in North Carolina.

April 3, 1865 - Union troops occupy Richmond and Petersburg, Virginia.

April 6, 1865 - The Battle of Sailor's Creek, Virginia. A portion of Lee's Army- almost one-third of it — is cornered along the banks of Sailor's (or "Saylor's") Creek and annihilated.

April 9, 1865 - Battle of Appomattox Court House and Surrender, Appomattox Court House, Virginia. After an early morning attempt to break through Union forces blocking the route west to Danville, Virginia, Lee seeks an audience with General Grant to discuss terms. That afternoon in the parlor of Wilmer McLean, Lee signs the document of surrender. On April 12, the Army of Northern Virginia formally surrenders and is disbanded.

April 14, 1865 - President Abraham Lincoln is assassinated by actor John Wilkes Booth at Ford's Theater in Washington, DC. On the same day, Fort Sumter, South Carolina is re-occupied by Union troops.

April 26, 1865 - General Joseph Johnston signs the surrender document for the Confederate Army of the Tennessee and miscellaneous southern troops attached to his command at Bennett's Place near Durham, North Carolina.

May 4, 1865 - General Richard Taylor surrenders Confederate forces in the Department of Alabama, Mississippi and East Louisiana.

May 10, 1865 - Confederate President Jefferson Davis is captured near Irwinville, Georgia.

May 12, 1865 - The final battle of the Civil War takes place at Palmito Ranch, Texas. It is a Confederate victory.

May 23, 1865 - The Grand Review of the Army of the Potomac in Washington, D.C.

May 24, 1865 - The Grand Review of General Sherman's Army in Washington, D.C.

May 26, 1865 - General Simon Bolivar Buckner enters into terms for the surrender of the Army of the Trans-Mississippi, which are agreed to on June 2, 1865. The Civil War officially ends.[9]

The Design of the Blockade Ship

The typical blockade-runner of 1863-4 was a long, low side-wheel steamer of from four to six hundred tons, with a slight frame, sharp and narrow, its length perhaps nine times its beam. It had feathering paddles, and one or two raking telescopic funnels, which might be lowered close to the deck. The hull rose only a few feet out of the water and was painted a dull gray or lead color so that it could hardly be seen by daylight at two hundred yards. Its spars wore two short lower-masts, with no yards, and only a small crow's-nest in the foremast. The deck forward was constructed in the form known as "turtle-back," to enable the vessel to go through a heavy sea. Without any diagrams or schematics, we do not know if the *Acadia* was a turtleback. Anthracite coal, which made no smoke, was burned in the furnaces. This coal came from the United States, and when, in consequence of the prohibition upon its exportation enforced by the Government, it could not be obtained, the semi-bituminous Welsh coal was used as a substitute. When running in, all lights were put out, the binnacle and fire-room hatch were carefully covered, and steam was blown off under water. In the latest vessels of this class,

The boiler of the USS *Westfield*.[11] The boilers were huge as seen in the Texas City Museum.

speed was too much studied at the expense of strength, and some of them were disabled before they reached their cruising-ground.[10]

1864 Blockade-Runner
Acadia Built in Sorel, Québec, Canada

Scotland could barely keep up with their orders to build blockade-runners. With rich forestlands nearby, Sorel, Quebec became a hub for building blockade-runners and other steamships. It was the fourth oldest city in Quebec. Sorel-Tracy, the town's name was once William-Henry and changed back to Sorel in 1845.

Sorel-Tracy is a city in southwestern Quebec, Canada at the confluence of the Richelieu River and the St. Lawrence River, on the western edge of Lac Saint-Pierre. The city is the result of the amalgamation of several communities, including Sorel, Tracy, and Saint-Pierre-de-Sorel.[13]

SINCENNES (Saincennes), JACQUES-FÉLIX, shipowner, businessman, and politician; b. in Deschambault, Hampshire County (Portneuf), L.C., 7 Jan. 1818, son of Jacques Saincennes, a farmer and pilot, and Marie-Josephte Marcotte; d. at Montreal, Que., 20 Feb. 1876.

The Saint-Seine family were Acadians, who had originally come from the village of Bourguignon, near the source of the Seine in France. At the time of the expulsion of the Acadians, they settled on the north shore of the St. Lawrence, and the name became first Saincennes and then Sincennes, which is the form Jacques-Félix used. At the age of 13, after six years at

J.F. Sincennes, owner/partner of the *Acadia*.

school, he was apprenticed to his father as a pilot and for two years plied the St. Lawrence between Quebec and Montreal. He then returned to school to finish his education and was thereafter employed as a clerk in a commercial house, before he obtained the post of purser in 1839 on a Montreal-Laprairie steamer.

Sincennes soon realized that one of the great needs of the region was a steamship service on the Richelieu River to carry produce from Chambly to William-Henry (Sorel) and on to Montreal: a 90-mile route in all. In 1845 he held a series meetings of the Richelieu habitants, at such centres as Saint-Charles-sur-Richelieu, at which subscriptions were raised to the value of £3,715; this amount was used to build the side-wheeler *Richelieu* (the first ship built at the Sorel shipyards) and the barge *Sincennes*. The new company was called *"La Société de Navigation de la Rivière Richelieu."* Sincennes became the captain, in which capacity he not only transported produce, but soon performed the apparently impossible task of moving square timber from William-Henry to Chambly.

Almost immediately a rival line was formed and the first of many amalgamations took place, resulting in the Richelieu Company (*La Compagnie du Richelieu*), which was incorporated by statute in 1848. The founders and stockholders were all French and French was the language in which the entire business of the company was conducted until 1875. By 1848 operations had so expanded that Sincennes gave up the captaincy to conduct the shore business; he was secretary-treasurer of the company for many years, president for a decade, and a director until his death. His policy was one of continued expansion and, when competition broke out, amalgamation with his rivals. In 1856 the company launched the Victoria and the Napoléon and entered the hotly contested Montreal-Quebec run in rivalry with the Molson, Torrance, and Tate interests [see Torrance]. At the same time it took over the fleet of the Montreal and Three Rivers Navigation Company. In 1857 the Richelieu Company was capitalized by statute at £75,000 and in that year it paid a 32 per cent dividend. The next year the Torrance interests were incorporated into the company and David Torrance became a director, thus ending the competition.

In 1860 the expanded organization made a profit-pooling agreement with the Toronto-Montreal Royal Mail Line to prevent competition. The St. Lawrence North Shore Navigation Company was taken over in that same year and the Lake St Peter Navigation Company and the Terrebonne and L'Assomption Navigation Company in 1861. By this time "in many cases the season's operations resulted in gross earnings greater than the total capital of the company," which by 1861 was $161,733. In 1862 the charter of the Richelieu Company was extended to permit operations throughout the St. Lawrence and the Great Lakes. The final amalgamation with which Sincennes was involved came in 1875, after a period of rivalry, when the Richelieu Company joined with the Canadian Navigation Company (formerly the Royal Mail Line) of Sir Hugh Allan to found the Richelieu and Ontario Navigation Company (from 1913 Canada Steamship Lines), which operated a total of 18 ships on the Great Lakes and St. Lawrence and had a paid up capital of $750,000. Sincennes remained a director of the new corporation.

While establishing the Richelieu Company, Sincennes was also involved with another important shipping operation. In 1849 he and William McNaughton, whose interests lay in Ottawa valley lumber and forwarding, formed a partnership, the Sincennes-McNaughton Line (today McAllister Towing Limited).

2, rue Charlotte et 88, rue de la Reine, Sorel-Tracy

With headquarters at Sorel and Montreal, this company specialized in towing berthing ships, as well as towing timber rafts and lumber barges on the Ottawa, Richelieu, and St Lawrence rivers, as far east as Quebec. The tugs used were of the side-wheel type. Sincennes was the president in what must have been an amicable relationship, for he and McNaughton were also engaged in various other partnerships such as the Montreal and Ottawa Forwarding Company, formed in 1865.

Sincennes took part in many other commercial and financial enterprises: in 1873, with McNaughton and others, he founded the Royal Canadian Insurance Company of Montreal and at the end of its first year became president. By 1875 the company had 300 agencies in Canada and the United States. He was, in addition, vice-president of *La Banque du Peuple* and was involved with companies manufacturing cotton and India-rubber goods.[16]

The "Acadia" Mail Carrier

The Sincennes-McNaughton Line added the 1,077-ton side-wheeler *Acadia*, newly-built at Sorel, to the route. In 1864 it was the steamer *Acadia* carried mails up and down the river for a short time. "Built expressly for the route," trumpeted one newspaper. Her arrival was greeted with the press's usual optimism and high expectations of "supplying the wants of commerce with the Lower Provinces." As far as can be determined, she lasted only until August . . . On September 7, she cleared for Halifax, which she reached eleven days later.

Front of Sincennes-McNaughten Building.[14]

Sincennes-McNaughten Headquarters

The *Acadia* made only two voyages from Quebec, one on July 21 to Pictou and a second to Shediac, and suffered an enormous loss, for the time, of $8,000. She was therefore withdrawn and, like the *Arabian* three years before, went south, sailing to Havana, to be used as a blockade-runner between Nassau and Charleston. A second 612-ton *Acadia* was built at Hamilton for other owners in 1867 but spent all her three decades trading between Montreal and Great Lakes ports for the Merchants' Line of Montreal.[17]

Sincennes was an important politician and businessman. McNaughton was in the forestry industry. The boats from their company were sailing on the great lakes, Ottawa River, St-Laurence River and Richelieu River between Montréal and Toronto. Sorel shipyard is now called Marine Industry Ltd.[18]

Many navigation companies were active in the towing of rafts and wood barges. Around 1867, for instance, Sincennes and McNaughton operated a fleet of seven steam-boats and 30 barges.[19]

Nautical Specifications for the Acadia

REGISTRATION CERTIFICATE OF THE ACADIA

PUBLIC ARCHIVES OF CANADA,
RECORD GROUP 42, VOLUME 117, NO. 154

Les Bateaux de la Cie Sincenne Mc Noughton dans le port de Sorel, P. Q.

The shipyard where the *Acadia* was built.

SIGNAL LETTER - V. H. P. H.   NUMBER OF SHIP - 46.239

PORT NUMBER - 17 of 1864   PORT OF REGISTRY - MONTREAL

BRITISH BUILT - STEAM POWERED WITH PADDLEWHEELS.

BUILT IN SOREL, PROVINCE OF CANADA ON MAY 10, 1854

One Poop and promenade and Hurricane.

Two masts, Schooner Rigging, Round Stern, Carvel built no
No Gallery, no Head, wood Framework . . .

Measured by rules 2,

Length from the Foreport of the Stem under the Bowsprit to the Aft

Side of the Head of the Sternpost ——— 211 Feet 11 Inches

Main Breadth to Outside of Plank ————— 31 Feet 1 Tenth

Depth in Hold from Tonnage Dock of Ceiling at Midships   12 Feet 6
Tenths

REGISTER TONNAGE ——738.45

ONE ENGINE, 900 Horsepower 81 Feet 11 Tenths Engineroom

JOINT OWNERS

Jacques Felix Lincennes.(*sic*)   Of Sorel, Province of Canada.
William McNaughten.   Of Montreal

DATED

14th July, 1864

ACTION: TITLE DERIVED FROM JACQUES F. LINCENNES (*SIC*)

WM. McNAUGHTEN - 64 SHARES

REGISTRY DATE: 31st OCTOBER 1864 - 1'CLOCK P.M.

CERTIFICATE OF SALE: DATED ———31st OCTOBER 1864.

THOMAS LEACH OF HALIFAX, MASTER OF THE "ACADIA" HAS IM-
POWERED TO SELL THE SHIP - NO MINIMUM PRICE NAMED, AT ANY
PLACE OUT OF THE PROVINCE OF CANADA WITHIN 12 MONTHS
FROM DATE OF CERTIFICATE . . .

SHIP WRECKED IN THE GULF OF MEXICO NEAR VELASCO IN 1864.
CERTIFICATE MOT RETURNED.

REGISTRY CLOSED: 9 FEBRURY 1866.

A STEAMBOAT RACE

Ross's Weekly

August 12, 1864

The statement in the last *(Ross's) Weekly* that there had been "a race between the Steamer *Princess of Wales* and the Quebec steamer *Acadia*, for $150, is incorrect. The

Drawing similar to the deck of the *Acadia*. The Blockade runner *Lillian*; American Civil War 1864.Sketch showing the steamship *Lillian* running the blockade into Wilmington Harbor, during the American Civil War. *Courtesy © Illustrated Long News Ltd/Mary Evans*

Acadia and the *Princess of Wales* were both in Shediac, the former bound up the Strait towards Miramichi, and the latter to Summerside, and as both were about to leave Port at the same hour, the *Acadia* got underway first and ran down the harbour a short distance, and waited a few minutes for the Princess to come up; and when the latter came abreast of the *Acadia*, both ran down the Harbour together, the *Princess* gaining on the *Acadia*. We are requested to state that "no race" took place, and that the Princess was not propelled beyond her ordinary speed.[22]

A STEAMBOAT RACE
Halifax Sun and Advertiser
AUGUST 17, 1864 PAGE 2

A RACE—We have been informed that a race for $150 came off yesterday between the *"Princess of Wales,"* and the new Quebec steamer *"Acadia"* which result-

Princess of Wales Steamer

ed in the bet being won by the former—*Ross Weekly*
(Charlottestown).

Subsidy Offered

Halifax Sun and Advertiser
Fri, Aug 26, 1864

> The Merchants of Miramichi have addressed a
> memorial to the Commissioner of Board of Works of
> New Brunswick, stating that they had examined the
> steamer *Acadia*, and pronounced her well adapted
> for the trade, and state that it will better subserve
> the interests of the northern section of the province,
> (if a subsidy is to be given) to run the boat between
> Quebec and Shediac, and intermediate ports, than by
> running her from Shediac to Dalhousie.[23]

ACADIA SOLD TO AMERICAN GENTLEMAN

August 27, 1864
Halifax Citizen, Halifax, Nova Scotia
Sat. Aug. 27, 1864 Page 2

The steamer *Acadia* built for the Gulf trade and intended to ply between that city and the lower New

Brunswick ports is to be withdrawn, the owners not being able to effect a satisfactory arrangement with the New Brunswick government. The Miramichi *Gleaner* says the Chief Commissioner of Works has offered a subsidy to the *Acadia* at the rate of (?) 1,500 a year, which the government has sanctioned, but her proprietors decline accepting it. Montreal papers of late date say that she sank $8000 in the two trips she made, and that she has been sold to an American, who is having her coppered, and altered for a sea voyage, and that she will sail for Halifax and Bermuda early in September.[24]

August 29, 1864
Halifax Sun and Advertiser
Halifax, Nova Scotia
Mon. Aug. 29, 1864 – Page 2

The Montreal *Telegraph* states that the steamer *Acadia* has been withdrawn from the Gulf trade, $3000 having been sunk in the two trips she made. This fine new steamer was sold on the 16th inst. to an American gentleman, is being coppered and altered for a sea voyage, and will leave Montreal with passengers in a few days for Halifax and Bermuda.

August 13, 1864
Halifax Citizen
Tuesday September 13, 1864 Page 3

Monday, September 12 –Steamers *Acadia* ---Quebec – flour to Maclean, Campbell and Co.

September 22, 1864, the following ad ran in the *Halifax Citizen*
SUPERFINE CANADA FLOUR
750 Barrels SUPERFINE FLOUR per steamer *Acadia* for sale by September 15, 1864 MACLEAN, CAMPBELL & CO

October 15, 1864
Halifax Citizen

Sat. Oct 15, 1864 Page 2

The Steamer *Acadia* – The steamer *Acadia* has not sold, as was announced by a contemporary last evening. It is understood that the owners will dispose of her if they will receive a suitable offer, but if no purchaser offers within a short time she will be sent to Havana for a market.[25]

In Large Marine Cradle Slip at Dartmouth October 30, 1864

Halifax Sun and Advertiser
Halifax, Nova Scotia
Monday Oct 30, 1864 Page 2

Mr. Crandell has succeeded in fitting the cradle of the large marine slip at Dartmouth in working order again. The steamer Acadia is now on it.

Substitute for *Acadia*

The *Quebec News* says the splendid side-wheel steamer Osprey, Capt. Paterson will leave this port for Halifax, N.S., calling at the unusual intermediate stopping places, on or about the 14th inst. The *Osprey* is quite new with excellent accommodation for freight and passengers and will prove an excellent substitute for the *Acadia*, which was found too expensive a boat to keep on the line. She was built to play on the upper lakes and is a staunch and thorough sea-going vessel on every respect. It is the intention of her owners to place her permanently on the route between Quebec and the lower port next season. All information can be obtained from her agent, Mr. W. Crawford, at his office, Crawford's wharf.[26]

Government Printing Office

1896 Official records of three Union and Confederate Navies

in the War of the Rebellion. Series I, Vol. 3:393-394

Letter from the U.S, Consul at Halifax, Nova Scotia, to the

Assistant Secretary of State, reporting the formation of a

Confederate Organization for the purpose

of destroying American commerce.

Hon. FEWSWEICK W. SEWARD,

Assistant Secretary of State

The Confederate war relied on the bravery of the "blockade runners" a small group of sailors from Europe and Canada and other ports who brought much-needed goods to the Southern seaports under the guns of the Union ships.

Brazoria County Historical Museum, found the following in unpublished letters.

Dec. 25th 1863, Velasco, Texas
WHAT GREAT-GRANDPA SAID TO G R E A T - G R A N D M A
(Copies of letters written by Dr. Thomas B. Grayson, a surgeon during the Civil War, to his wife, Carrie, during the years of 1863, 1664, and 1665)

During the past ten or twelve days, quite a number of schooners have run the blockade at this port. A majority of them, so Madam Rumor says, are loaded with guns, ammunition and army stores for "Old Jeff". On Wednesday the Yankees played quite "a trick" on our pilots. A schooner came in sight and as is usual with the "blockade running", made signal for a pilot. Those pilots, not thinking but what it was a vessel desiring to come into our port, jumped in a yawl and went out to them, when to their great surprise they found that it was a Yankee boat. They took the pilots on board, carried them out on sea some thirty miles when they allowed them to take the yawl and make to shore if they could, which they succeeded in doing about 12 o'clock last night. They in future, will I guess, be rather particular before they board another boat. A courier came in last evening with a dispatch to Genl. Suckett that a schooner loaded with guns and powder was beached on the coast some eighteen miles from here and that the Yankee Gunboat was cruising around and evidently meditated her destruction. A large detail was sent down (here about half a line is torn too badly to decipher) protect her. Among the number are Charlie, Frank Daniel, and Gid

Walker. They had to walk, of course, carrying their guns and 40 rounds of ammunition. I came near being sent myself. I would not be surprised they did not have a brush with the Yankees. The poor fellows are right tired this morning, after having walked all night. Two wagons loaded with guns and ammunition have just come in from the vessel. They report the Yankee Gunboat 4 miles off.

The Ports of Halifax and Saint John and the American Civil War

"Running the Blockade"
Halifax Sun November 7, 1864
Now landed safely in Halifax, the dangers we have
passed enhanced all our pleasures — too dear
alas! to last
From ladies' hearts and shopmen's arts, resistance is
not made — We'll spend our gold, like Timon of old,
while "Running the Blockade" So fill our glass to every
lass, of every hue and shade
Who takes her stand, for Dixie's land
And Running the Blockade.

Letter from the U.S. Consul at Halifax, Nova Scotia, to the assistant Secretary of State, reporting the formation of a Confederate organization for the purpose of destroying American commerce.[28]

Consulate of the United States of America
Halifax Nova Scotia, December 13, 1864
Sir: I have the honor to inform you that an organization of rebels has been formed, consisting of at least 300 persons, for the purpose of seizing, plundering, destroying and, when practice, approaching American steamers and other vessels at different points along the Atlantic and Pacific coasts and on the upper lakes.
The main object of the pirates will be to seize vessels having large amounts of money on board.
This body of desperadoes will separate into smaller parties and operate at different points.
Their base of operations and headquarters will be at Havana, at which place they will be supplied with money and such arms and other measures as may be necessary to facili-

tate their operations.

A portion of the company may remain at Nassau, another portion will proceed from Havana to Vera Cruz, and another portion will go to California for the purpose of intercepting and seizing the Pacific mail steamers.

The steamers conveying the largest amounts of money will be the special objects of attack.

Several persons belonging to the organization have commissions from the rebel Secretary of the Navy.

Some of the parties connected with this pirates gang left here last week in the steamer *Acadia*, which sailed for Nassau and Havana, and which steamer, it is said, will proceed from Havana to Vera Cruz.

Lieutenant Braine (sic Brain),[29] one of the Piratical leaders, who also was connected with the seizer of the Chesapeake and Roanoke, and also has a commission from the rebel Government, was here two or three days ago in disguise and left under an assumed name in a schooner for Nassau.

McDonald who was connected with Briane (sic Brain)[30] in the seizure of the Chesapeake, is said to be in Canada, in the vicinity of Detroit.

I have the honor to be your obedient servant

M.M. Jackson　　U.S. Consul.on. Frederic W. Seward

Assistant Secretary of State.

This River Clyde type steamship was built at Sorel, Quebec, Canada, on May 10, 1864, by B of D and I. Mc Eritly, Sorel.

Port No 17 of 186　No. of ship　46.239

Signal letter　V.H.P.M.

One poop and one promenade and Hurricane
Two masts, Schooner Rigging, Round Stern, Carvel built, no Gallery, no Head, metal-clad wood Framework

Depth in hold from Tonnage Deck of ceiling at midships, 12 Feet 6 Tenths

Owners Jacques Felix Sincennes, Sorel, and William McNaughton, Montreal.[31]

Newspaper Articles

Halifax Citizen
November 17, 1864[32]
Steam to Nassau, N.P. and Havana
    The powerful new side-wheel British Steamer
"Acadia" Thomas Leach Commander, will
leave Halifax, N.S. for above ports on or about
November 9, 1864. The *"Acadia"* has unsurpassed
accommodations for cabin passengers.
    For freight or passage, apply to the Master
on board, or at the office of the agents, Jerusalem Warehouse:
Oct 22   MACLEAN CAMPBELL & CO

CAPAIN JOHN C. BRAINE (*sic* Brain)[33] A Privateer, he was duly commissioned and had a Letter of Marque. He boarded the *Acadia* in Halifax on her maiden voyage to Havana.

JOHN BRAINE(sic Brain)[34] *DEAD*

Famous Figure in Confederate Navy Expires at Tampa.

Tampa, Fla. — John C Braine (*sic* Brain)[35] of the Confederate navy died here today of paralysis. During the Civil war he commanded several confederate vessels. After the war he went to England and returning a year later he was arrested by order of the Secretary of the Navy Gideon Well, and was held a prisoner until March, 1869, being the last Confederate prisoner to be released.[36]

Having been a forgotten prisoner in the Brooklyn Penitentiary, he became known as the "Man without a Country."He clearly states his name was spelled "Brain." He was the last prisoner of war and the last American privateer.

STEAMER ACADIA

In Large Marine Cradle at Dartmouth, Nova Scotia to be
Coppered   October 30, 1864

Cleared Customs Halifax, Nova Scotia November 29, 1864
Sailed from Halifax   December 6, 1864

Entered Bermuda   December 12, 1864
Cleared Bermuda   December 13, 1864

Arrived Nassau   December 19, 1864
Cleared Nassau   December 20, 1864

Arrived Havana   December 22, 1864
Cleared Havana   January 25, 1865

Wreck   February 6, 1865
Near San Luis Pass, Texas

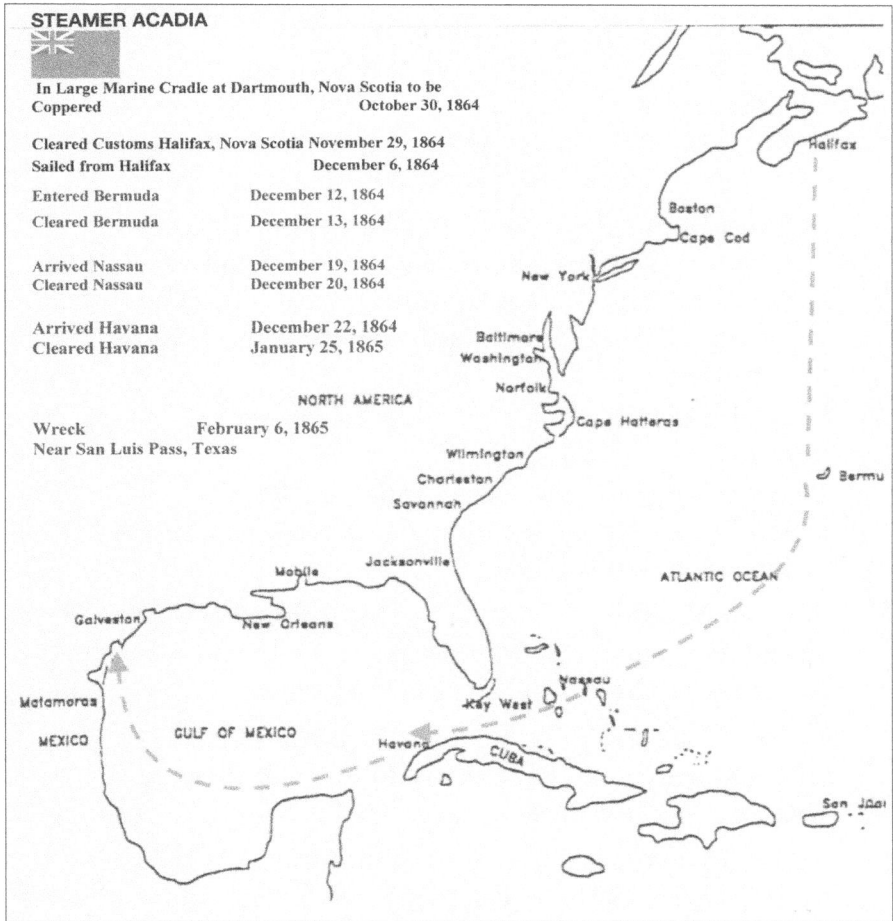

Acadia Map Route

Acadia Map Timeline Route[37] Dates taken From Newspaper
Articles 1864-1865.

Halifax Citizen
December 3, 1864

Cleared[38] Halifax Nova Scotia   November 29, 1864
Steamer *Mavrocordatos*, Smith, Liverpool, G.B. by B Wier
& Co., Steamer *Acadia*, Leach, Nassau, **N P. by P Walsh**
and others

Sailed from Halifax   December 6, 1864
After many delays, the steamer *Acadia* sailed today at

noon for Nassau and Havana taking special mails for these places.[39]

Royal Gazette
Bermuda Commercial and General Advertiser and Recorder
CUSTOMS HOUSE ST. GEORGE

Entered Bermuda   December 12, 1864
December 12—Steamer *Acadia*, ——, Halifax — five days: called here for coal, bound for Havana. The *Acadia* is to be employed in trading between Havana and Matamoras.

Dec. 13, 1864[40]

Bermuda Royal Gazette
Cleared Bermuda   December 13, 1864[41]
Sailed December 13, steamer *Acadia*, for Nassau
01 Jan. 1865 issue

Arrived Nassau   December 19, 1864
Str. *Acadia*, Leach, merchandise & c., to Johnson & Brother.
The Nassau Guardian Dec. 21, 1864 issue

Cleared Nassau   December 20, 1864
Str. *Acadia*, Leach, mchdse., by Johnson & Brother.
The Nassau Guardian Dec. 21, 1864 issue

Arrived Havana   December 22, 1864
New York Times Reported the *Acadia* at Havana, Cuba
Dec. 24, 1864.
By the steamer *Acadia*, which arrived here the day before yesterday (Dec. 22) from Nassau, news of a very recent date has been received from Charleston.[42]

Buffalo Morning Express
Reported the steamer *Acadia* arrived at Havana from Halifax: supposed intended for a blockade-runner. Dec. 30, 1864[43]

Hartford Courant-The Daily Courant
The steamer *Acadia* had arrived at Havana from Halifax, supposed to be intended for a blockade runner.[44]
Dec 30, 1864

Madison Courier, Madison, Indiana Feb. 8, 1865
Cleared Havana   **January 25, 1865**
The Steamer *Acadia* cleared at Havana ostensibly for Bermuda, with a cargo of three hundred and twenty kegs of gun-powder, bar iron, rope, &c.
The steamer sailed on the 25th for Galveston.[45]

Although Dr. Wendell Pierce indicated the main group of passengers stayed in Havana and made their headquarters there to meet with their leader Lt. Braine (*sic*). The rest of the passengers went on to Vera Cruz where they disembarked to go overland for the Pacific Ocean to raid mail carriers near California. From there the *Acadia* left for Galveston. Nowhere can I confirm this statement.

In a very dense fog, the *Acadia* ran hard aground the night of February 6, 1865, near San Luis Pass, Texas.

Galveston Weekly News, Feb. 15, 1865[46]
The loss of three Confederate steamers and on our coast, within the last two or three days will, probably remind our readers of the following article, which we published on the 25th ult.:

IMPORTANT FROM NASSAU - The *Charleston Mercury*, of Dec. 13th says: "The following extract of a private letter from Nassau conveys a very important hint. I am of the opinion that during this winter, blockade-runners will have more to fear from enemies in their own crews than they will have from the blockading fleet. Hundreds of Yanks are now here, and I suspect that it is a settled plan to capture vessels by a stratagem at sea. Spies are all around, and it may be that you will hear of several Roanoke affairs this next moon. An attempt was thus made to capture the *Owl*, which failed, and eight of the crew are now in irons, one of them holding a Yankee commission as Master's Mate. This looks serious, but proper precautions, on the part of the officers, will render these devilish plans abortive. Owing to the dubious character of English neutrality, these mercenary minions of the tyrannical Yankee Government will escape punishment."

There is hardly any room to doubt that the three steamers were wrecked on our coast by Yankees in disguise. We learn that they are in the streets of Havana, disguised as British sailors, seeking an opportunity to ship on blockade-runners. We fear the commanders of these unfortunate steamers have been caught in the trap set for them. We should never forget that treachery, falsehood and deception are the peculiar characteristics of Yankees, and we believe we have more to fear from these traits than from all their power in open and honorable war. It should be remembered that the coast of Texas is the safest of any on the whole seaboard of this continent. The water shoals so gradually and so uniformly that, with the lead and line in the hands of any but a Yankee, no blockade runner could be beached in the thickest fog, unless intentionally. We have no doubt that the loss of the *Wisp*, the *Wren* and the *Arcadia* [sic., Acadia] is due to Yankee treachery. The lesson has been dearly bought, but we hope we shall profit by it.

Cleveland Leader
Published
Daily, Tri-Weekly and Weekly
March 1, 1865
The Navy Department has information that the side-wheel steamer *Acadia* is lying a wreck, riddled by shot and shell from the United States steamer *Virginia*, six miles from Velasco, where she ran ashore after several attempts to get into that port.[47]

Royal Gazette
Bermuda Commercial and General Advertiser and Recorder
Hamilton, Bermuda. Tuesday, March 14, 1865

The steamer *Acadia* was destroyed while attempting to run the blockade at Velasco, by the U.S. steamer *Virginia*. The *Acadia* was built as a packet boat from Quebec to ports in New Brunswick and Nova Scotia. She was on her first trip.[48]

Captain Thomas Leach of Halifax, first and only captain.

Galveston Tri-Weekly
February 21, 1865

LOSS OF THE STEAMSHIP *ACADIA*
by W. Jowrick

In the *Houston Daily Telegraph* of the 9th instant, appears a paragraph referring to the beaching of this fine steamer, stating that the cause of the misfortune was owing to the sailing master's want of intimate knowledge of the currents. Allowing such to be the case, what excuse can be offered for running the ship among the breakers, in that foggy weather? After the lookout forward had reported several times breakers ahead, and on both bows, her head was still standing inshore, and the soundings had been regularly given from five, down to two fathoms, and then eleven feet. When the ship had reached soundings, the sailing master had given up command.

The coast tends in a straight line from San Luis Pass along Galveston Island; and had the ship been ten or twelve miles to the eastward of her present position, and in eleven feet soundings, her head in-shore the same, or N.E., she would have struck, and probably met with a similar result; therefore her being to the West was not the cause. The paragraph alluded to also states that she was thirty miles west of her recording. Such is not the case; my instructions from the pilot were to make the land twelve or fifteen miles to the west of Galveston, and I accordingly shaped a course that would bring her to the No. of latitude 29"9′ deg.; No. of long., 94:54 W.; but either owing to the strong west current, and steering, or the inefficient (I may say) useless manner in which the compasses were fixed, she drifted to the West, no regard being had for quantity of iron and iron nails closely connected with the needle, in fact, not a binnacle in the ship, the compasses not even fixed on deck when leaving Havana; though I often demonstrated and pointed out the caution that was necessary, to prevent as much as possible the uncertain direction of the needle, when influenced by too close a proximity to iron. During the last few days, two steamers left Havana on the same voyage as the *Acadia*, and both were driven to the West- on in particular, (the *Wren*) several miles farther than ourselves. They no doubt had good navigators on board who, were also well acquainted with the Gulf and its currents; it is not to be supposed they were all mistaken either in their navigation or chronometers, and the conclusion to be arrived at is that some unusually strong wind set to the West, was experienced by all; and I understand the general opinion among coasters is that the current ebbs with the wind, on a N. and N.E. wind to S. and W. On the 1st and 2nd instant, we had a fresh breeze from S.E. to S.W. This, according to their theory, would not cause a set to West or South of West. After the lookout forward had reported breakers ahead, she struck (the last soundings being 11 feet.) The engine was reversed, and she backed off with good way into deep water. The order was then given to go ahead, when she again struck, the concussion causing the bursting of the steam pipe, rendering the machinery useless. A report has also been spread that the cause of her going ashore was losing her rudder and becoming unmanageable. The rudder did not give way till some hours after she had been laying on the beach, broadside on the sea. I think it only just to those who were on board at the time, and owners, to lay these facts before the public. I do not blame anyone in particular, but do not believe the whole weight should be thrown on the shoulders of the sailing master.

Her first and only Captain, Thomas Leach picked up cargo in Nassau and then headed to Velasco. They sailed along the coast to avoid Federal Blockade ships. In the night of February 5, 1865, a heavy fog sat in along the coast and she ran aground in 15-feet of water near San

Luis Pass. There were no serious injuries or damage, but she was stuck beyond hope. Word was sent to the forts at Quintana and Velasco for help. The coastal patrol came and by daylight, most of the cargo was unloaded. Gunfire from the *USS Virginia* disabled the *Acadia* as daylight came. Her cargo consisted of marble doorknobs, brass locks, keys, brass lamps, large jars, olives, and spirits.

Nearby Confederate Military Forts[50]

Word was sent to the forts of Quintana and Velasco for help from the Coastal patrol.

The Texas coast was a division of the Western Gulf Blockading Squadron.

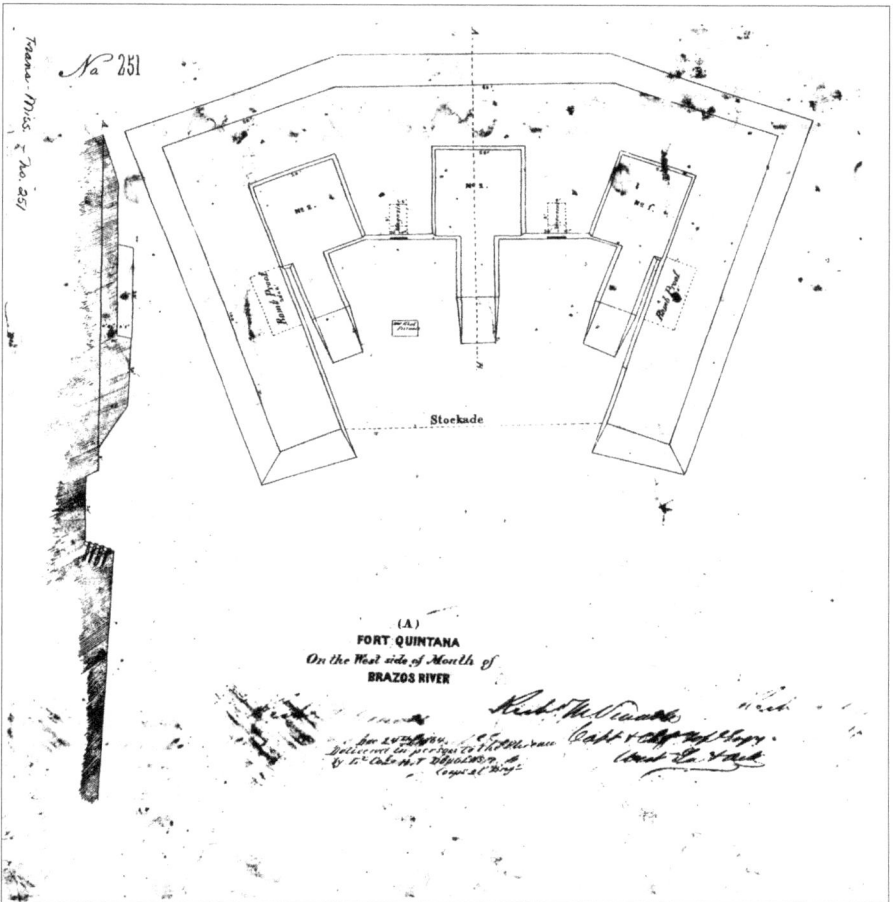

Fort Quintana[51]

Military Facilities in Texas 1861-1865

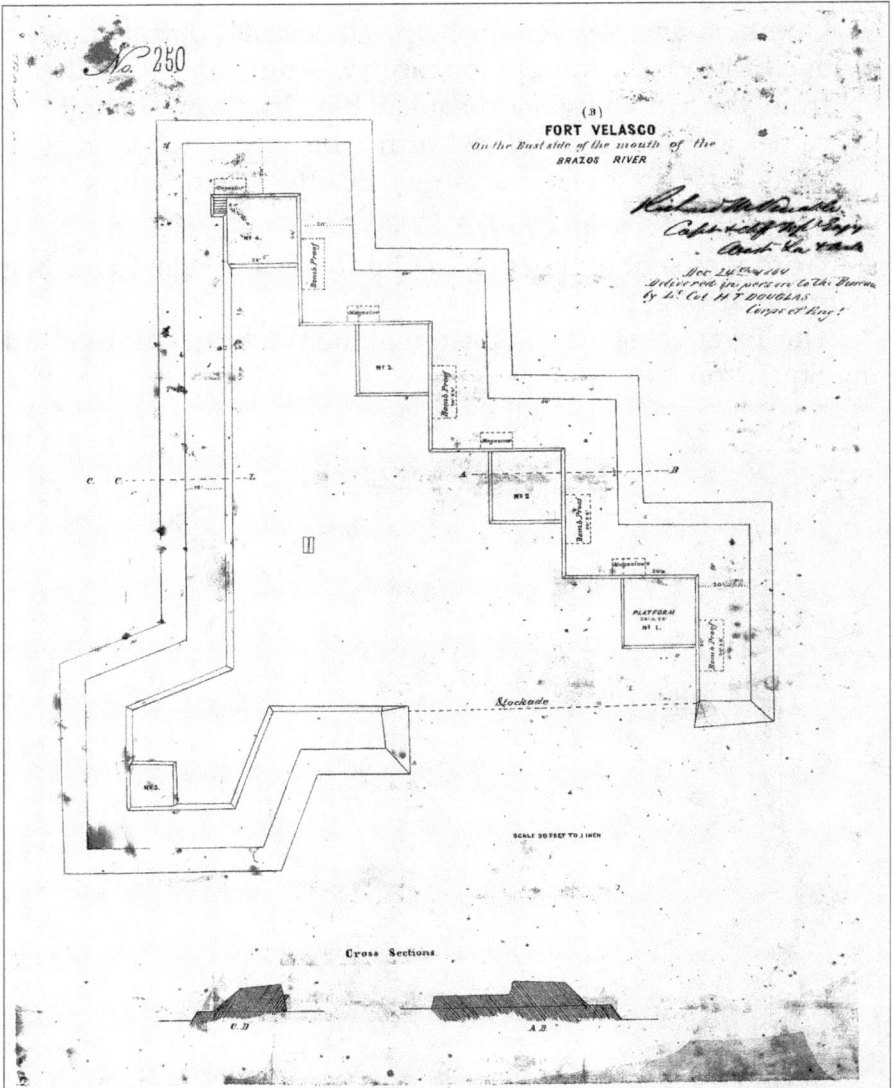

Fort Velasco[52] – Located on the northeast bank of the mouth of the Brazos River. Armament at this earthwork consisted of 6-24 pounder smoothbores, 1-8 inch howitzer, and 1-32 pounder naval gun. Fort Velasco, Fort Sabine and Fort Derby are similar design—all drawn by Julis G. Kellersberger.

U.S.S. Virginia

The third Virginia was originally the British merchantman *Pet* built at Dumbarton, Scotland, in 1861. *Pet* sailed as *Noe-*

Daquy during the early months of the Civil War and, in December 1862, was acquired by a Havana merchant for use as a Confederate blockade-runner. Renamed *Virginia*, the vessel was captured off Mugeres Island, Mexico, by *Wachusett* and *Sonoma* on 18 January 1863; was later purchased by the Navy from the New York prize court on 1 September; and was commissioned at the New York Navy Yard on 12 June.

Virginia was assigned duty with Rear Admiral David G. Farragut's West Gulf Blockading Squadron and, within a week of her commissioning, departed New York, bound for the Gulf of Mexico. En route, she touched briefly at Hampton Roads, Virginia, finally joining Farragut's squadron in July. However, further repairs and modifications were needed before the vessel could become a fully effective fighting unit; and the ship spent August and most of September at New Orleans undergoing overhaul.

Virginia finally returned to active duty in late September and was deployed along the coast of Texas for the duration of the war. There, she conducted numerous patrol and reconnaissance missions, which often took her up the rivers which empty into the gulf, and also compiled an impressive list of captures. Her first success was the seizure of the British blockade-runner Jenny off the Texas coast with a cargo of cotton on 6 October. Between 2 and 14 November, *Monongahela*, *Owasco*, and *Virginia* convoyed and supported General Nathaniel Banks' successful landing at Brazos Santiago, Texas, near the mouth of the Rio Grande River. Here, *Virginia* also captured the British steamer *Matamoras* on the 4th and the English brig *Dashing Wave* on the 5th. This expedition began a Union offensive aimed both at wresting Texas from Confederate control and deterring French troops in Mexico from attempting to invade the state. On the 4th, Southern forces evacuated Brownsville, giving the Union a strong foothold at the Mexican border.

After the Rio Grande expedition, *Virginia* returned to blockade duty and found the waters off Texas a fertile breeding ground of smuggling activity. This was especially true of the area off San Luis Pass, Texas, and *Virginia* made most of her captures here. These included the British schooner *Mary Douglas* and her cargo of coffee, bananas, and linen, which were seized on 15 February 1864, and the English

schooner *Henry Colthirst* which she took on the 22nd. On the
29th off Galveston, Texas, *Virginia* overhauled the Confederate
schooner *Camilla* with a cargo of cotton. The sloop Cassie
Holt was also captured at the same time, but she grounded
off San Luis Pass and was burned. Once again off San Luis
Pass, *Virginia* captured the sloop *Randall* on 8 March, the
schooner *Sylphide* on the 10th, and the Mexican schooner
Juanita on 11 April. However, *Juanita* grounded on the 13th and
was recaptured with the loss of the prize crew. This incident
was partially offset by the capture of the Mexican schooner
Alma on the 19th and the seizure and destruction of the sloop
Rosina on the 20th. *Virginia's* last captures off San Luis Pass
included the schooner *Experiment*, which she took on 3 May
and subsequently destroyed and 94 stacked bales of cotton
picked up ashore on the 7th and 8th.

   Virginia returned to New Orleans in mid-May for
badly needed repairs to her boilers. She remained at New
Orleans until December, leaving on the 5th for the blockade

The *Virginia* log.

More of the *Virginia* Log.

off Galveston. Here, she captured the schooner *Belle* on 27 December and helped to destroy the side-wheel steamer *Acadia* in February 1865.After the war ended in April 1865, *Virginia* sailed for Philadelphia on 17 July. The veteran blockader was sold at public auction at New York City to Perry Brothers on 30 November; was documented on 14 December; and was re-rigged as a barge on 24 March 1885.

Published: Fri Oct 23 10:15:30 EDT 2015[53]

United States Steamer U.S.S. Virginia Log
Commanded by A.V. Lieut. C.H. Brown[54]

Their first thought was to send longboats but rifle fire from the shore stopped that.

The *Galveston Weekly News*
Wednesday, February 22, 1865

The Crew of the *U.S.S Virginia*

The *Philadelphia Inquirer,* Monday July 31, 1862

The United States Steamer *"Virginia,"* Galveston July

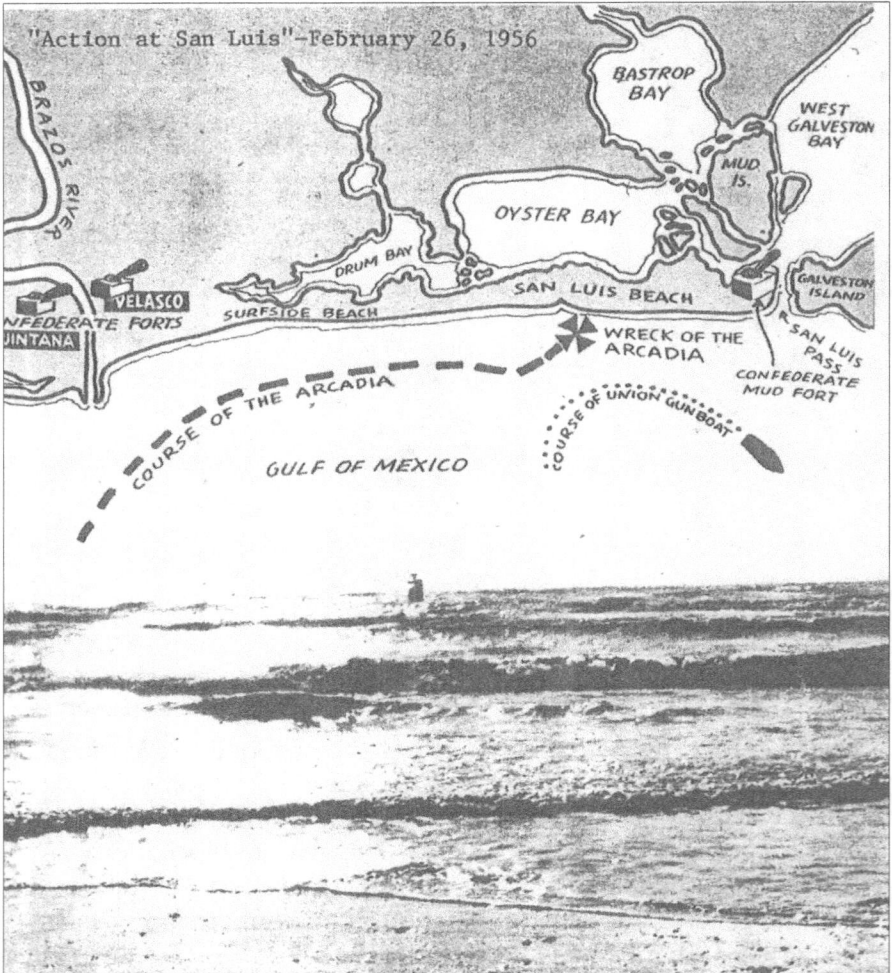

The rusting boiler of the blockade runner *Acadia* remains off San Luis Beach.
THE HOUSTON CHRONICLE ROTOGRAVURE MAGAZINE, SUNDAY, FEBRUARY 26, 1956

Approximate Location of Grounded *Acadia*.[55] *Brazosport Facts* March 13, 1966

13, via Pensacola, Tampa Bay and Key West, arrived at the Navy yard on Friday last. The is a list of her officers:—Acting Volunteer Lieutenant Charles. H Brown, commanding; Acting Master, W.G. Mitchell; Executive Officer, Acting Assistant Surgeon, W.H. Kinney; Acting Assistant Paymaster, J.B. Half; Second Assistant Engineer, J.D. Toppin, in charge; Acting Ensigns, F.E. Brockett and E.T. Small; Third Assistant Engineer, Daniel Ward,

James Esler and Jas. Scrib.

In an undated letter, A.F. Shannon told the following account to his son, L.C Shannon. A.F. Shannon saw the ship aground in 1865, when he was six-years-old. Captain Sterrett[56] stayed with A.F. Shannon's Uncle Lon (a Follett who lived with his mother Anne Louise Follett at Halfway House Hotel on Peninsula Point)[57] near San Luis.[58]

Houston Tri-Weekly Telegraph, February 10, 1865.[59]
Captain Sterrett arrived here on Tuesday night, bringing most of the cargo of the *Acadia* with him. He reported but a small portion of the cargo injured. The Vessel is high and dry on the beach and but little damaged. The cause of the misfortune was the want of intimate knowledge of the sailing master of the currents in the gulf, which put the vessel thirty miles out of his reckoning down the coast. She got in too near shore, and being well aware of the danger, the vessel struck bottom, breaking the connection pipe between the boilers. She then drifted to the beach.

Note: Telegraph to the *Galveston Daily News*, Saturday Oct. 14, 1865
Captain Sterrett delivered newspapers to Galveston from New Orleans. He owned to boats, the *Silver Cloud* which he commanded himself and the *St. Claire*. They moved commerce to and from Houston every other day except Sunday.

Houston Tri-Weekly Telegraph
11 Feb 1865
Acadia
We have had the pleasure of meeting with Mr. Simpson of Bay City Guard, Orderly Sergeant of that noble old company in 1863. He was captured at the battle of Gettysburg, and taken by the Yankees to Fort Delaware. He was confined at that fort until October 1863, when being sent on a buying detail, he managed to slip off and lose himself. He made his way at once to New York, where

his relatives and friends resided. To their entreaties and presumptions to stay with them and desert his adopted country, he replied that his country was the Confederacy, and there his duty would take him. He worked his way thence to Canada, and engaged there for the time in his business as engineer, waiting for a chance to come south.

Last summer Captain Sterrett arrived in Canada to buy a steamer, and sergeant Simpson at once sought him out, and engaged to ship with him for Texas as an engineer on his vessel. In this way he reached our coast on the *Acadia*.

Sergeant Simpson was one of the best soldiers of the old bayou City Guard, and like all of the company, stands true to the colors of his country. He has come back like a true man, to do his duty in the war, and he will do it wherever he is placed.[60]

Catalogue Sale of The Cargo of The Acadia

Reichman sold yesterday the entire cargo saved from the Steamer Acadia at the following prices: Brown domestic fine, 41.46 cents; brown drills 38-1/2 a 45; striped shirting, 31.39¢; English print 41, 41-1/2; red flannel $2; brown segath 75, 75-1/2 ¢; gray seathy, 61.70; Nova Scotia homespun wool 36-1/2 ¢; drab twill lining 24.25; drab fabric 34¢; figured sleeve lining 31 cents; drab twill 25-1/2 ¢; 11 dozen linnen hankerchiefs fine $4.14 per doz; silk do 80¢; flax thread $1.25 per pound; buttons $1.50 per gross; steel pins $1.75 per gross; official envelopes $5; letter paper $4.25; bill cap $4; lead pencils 8¢ each, $1.05 per doz; knives and forks damaged $1.85 and $2 per set; hand saws $15 per each; shingling hatchets $12 per doz; nail hammers $12 per dozen; Percussion caps $1.10.5.25; pocket knives $7.50.16 per doz; gray blankets $2 65.5 50; cotton cards $18.14 50 per doz; Round iron 11 ¢; flat bar 9-1/2; bailing twine, 13-1/2 20s; preserved fruit in cans $9.15 50 per doz; 34-1/2.35; nails $14.50; sweet oil per dozen quarts $6.

India bagging 30; Star Candles 31; Salt 2.3-1/2 per lb;

white lead $6.26 per keg of 25 lbs; Indigo $1.10; Black Tea $1; Claret $255; French letter paper $2.80; Cotton balhose $2.00; Blue Serge Shirts $1.10; Shoe thread 40 cents; Playing cards 45¢; Imperials 20.25 ¢; Gray Army cloth $175; Overshirts $1.25; Gold lace 15 ¢ per yard; Gray flannel $5; French Quinine $4.15; Calomel $3.25; Blue Mass, $2.15.

A portion of the goods were slightly damaged in getting them from the Acadia while the balance were in good condition. The few dozen preserved fruits, it will be seen, brought from four to five hundred per cent on first cost, while the necessary articles of iron brought but 10 ¢, but a trifle over actual cost, showing a proneness to indulge our appetites in preference to supplying the actual wants of the country.[61]

Information taken from War of the Rebellion by Mr. Charles W. Sterrett, the Western Gulf Squadron report; U.S.S. *Cayuga*, Off Galveston, Texas, March 27, 1865. Seven men from Colonel Joseph J. Cooks heavy artillery regiment stationed at Virginia Point, recovered most of the machinery from the *Acadia* and the *Will-of-the-Wisp*. They also made three guns from the shaft of the *Westfield*.[62]

The Civil War Ended April 9, 1865

The *Acadia* grounded in front of the Alexander Glass Follett's beach home on Follett's Island, four miles west San Luis Pass. As he watched from shore, in an 1886 letter to Judge H. P. Ballinger of Galveston, Alexander Glass Follett explained how the "Boiler Stacks" of the *Acadia* were iron and how well they held up from the pounding salt water surf.[63]

1865, October 3, Owner Thomas Leach, Halifax, Nova Scotia, to run Gulf of Saint Lawrence.[64]

1866 he became Captain of the *Rothsay Castle* for one year.[65]

Fisherman's Paradise

The "Boilers" nicknamed by the local fishermen was an absolute favorite spot for big fish. Myself being one of them, we would wade out to the second sandbar. We used a double clip brass snap release about three inches long to attach our live shrimp bait bucket and then clip it to our blue jean belt loop. This became our fish stringer and bait bucket line. Just in case a shark wanted our catch, we could do a quick release and head toward shore. And that did happen!

With nearly a fish limit on the stringer, my son-in-law was knocked underwater and when he came up—no stringer, fish or bait bucket! Just a short rope left.

Sincennes-McNaughton in May 2016 the headquarters burned. This may contribute to the fact there are no photos or schematics of the *Acadia*.[66]

Part Two

1969 Permit

Dr. T.E. Pulley, the curator of the Houston Museum of Natural Science held Permit No. 17 from the Texas Antiquities Committee for the purpose of carrying out archaeological investigation and recovery of artifacts from the wreck *Acadia*. Dr. Wendell E. Pierce worked very closely and was in constant contact with Dr. Pulley. Dr. Pulley displayed many artifacts in the Museum of Natural Science for years on the second floor.

Dr. Wendell E. Pierce, D.D.S. (nicknamed Dr. Magoo) recovered artifacts from the *Acadia*[68] from 1969 until his untimely death in 1973.

Wendell E. Pierce, D.D.S.

Among his many accomplishments in life, in 1943, Dr. Wendell E Pierce was a member of the Texas A&M, Texas Aggie (Field) Artillery Band. Also the Holland Lodge No.1 -Af&Am, Scottish Rite Bodies, Texas Dental Association, Houston Diving Club, First Baptist Church of Houston.

The mystery surrounding the *Acadia*, lying 300 yards offshore near San Luis Pass, Texas. Was she looted and stripped of her cargo? No one knew. In 1969 Dr. Pierce decided to find out for himself. Was there anything of historical value left?

How could such a light-weight craft remain upright during the 1900 and 1915 storms? Plus, others before and after? When she ran hard ashore, she hit a stratum of clay. Her nearly flat hull, designed to carry large loads in shallow water stuck to the clay almost like it was caught in concrete.

Well known, Dr. Wendell E. Pierce for his Gulf of Mexico-Caribbean Recovery Efforts.

Wendell recovered other artifacts in the Caribbean. One of his recovery

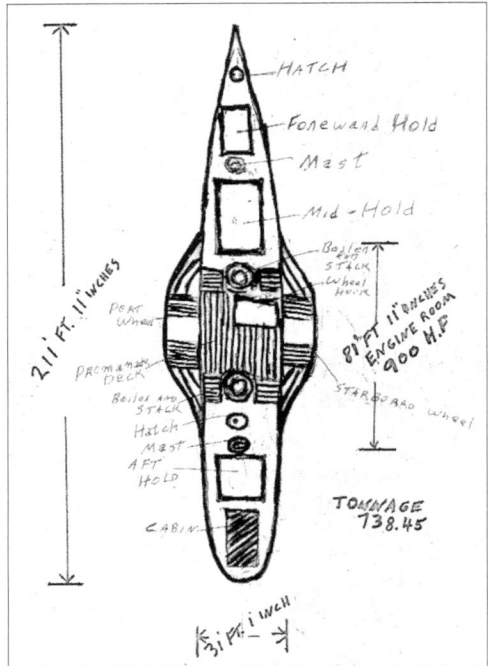

Line drawing by Dr. Wendell C. Pierce.

Line drawing Dr. Wendell C. Pierce

Dr. Wendell Pierce, a Houston dentist, surfaces after a dive in search of artifacts from the sunken Confederate ship. Pierce, an active scuba diver, has taken part in a number of underwater studies in the Gulf of Mexico.

The much discussed communication line in the hand of Dr. Pierce about to make a dive for artifacts on the *Acadia*.[68] Strong currents and murky water added a huge challenge.

sites was on the shipwreck the *El Matanceros*.[69]

Wendell joined up with Pablo Bush of CDAMM.[70]

All the artifacts were turned over to the museum in Mexico City and the Museum of Natural Science. Talk about lots of artifacts!!! Actual footage of the recovery of artifacts.[71]

References:

To the family of Pablo Bush Romero for permission to reprint chapter two of *Under the Waters of Mexico* and for many of the photos which appear here from the book. Two of the photos of Pablo Bush with club members and recovered cannons/artifacts are from the book *Mexican Caribbean* by Earl J. Wilson. [72]

WENDELL E. PIERCE. D.D.S.
2017 FANNIN STREET SUITE NO.4
HOUSTON, TEXAS 77004

Diving operations can be very difficult procedures if diving plans are not set up from the very beginning.

The diver or divers should start each diving day expecting the worst water conditions because it usually is.

Three hundred yards is a short distance with good condition, but in this surf, the lateral currents, are usually very strong.

First, and most, important step is to establish communication lines from the wreck to the shore. This can be done by taking an inexpensive cotton crap line 1/8 inch by over 1000 feet length the wreck with a float to the shore and secure it well with a chain or cable hooks. Return to the shore and secure it to a car or trailer, but I urge the use of a 1/4-inch nylon line. Another line should be secured to the stern and various other parts of the wreck where work is being done. In murky water these lines are is essential. Floats are necessary at each working area with artifact bags on each float. I used a rubber life raft and the other small boats when they were available. I had that luxury of a powerboat once. I am finding it much better to not depend on anyone and always be prepared to proceed each diving day with or without any help.

At first, these commutating lines may seem unnecessary but several times I found myself washed down the beach about a mile or more.

In the recovery of large or heavy artifacts, a 55-gallon oil drum should be sunk and secured to the artifact very tightly. With another air tank and pressure hose fill the old drum and a drum of this size should lift four hundred pounds. After reaching the surface hold on tightly to the communication line and allow the waves action to wash the artifacts and drum to shore. I always had a driftwood sled to put such artifacts on and drag them up to dry land.

Night diving is highly recommended because the water is usually a little more calmer but again the communication line is essential.

Artifacts consisting of ferrous metal should be submerged in fresh water immediately many times and mere fresh water should be changed several times. This takes a lengthy period of time but is necessary to revive the free chlorides from the metal. The water is treated with Silver nitrate.

Thorough drying by the sun or even an oven is necessary before spraying acrylic or plastic of the pores metal. This would be done slowly for over a period of days. This will completely seal off any atmospheric condition that may injure the metal.

Artifacts consisting of wood should be soaked in fresh water and changed every day making certain there are no chlorides and then boiled in water containing alum. Heat activated alum and penetrates ferrous artifacts; linseed oil and other wood preservatives can be administered to beautify the wood.

Brass or gold artifacts are the easiest to treat because they are not as vulnerable to electrolysis. By soaking in muriatic acid these metals are almost instantly cleaned and ready to polish if desired.[73]

Diving the Acadia with Wendell Pierce

I first met Dr. Pierce in the latter part of 1970 while I was attending commercial diving School at CDC in Houston. I was in class d-3, and Luther Swift one of my instructors was a friend of Dr. Pierce. Dr. Pierce was looking for divers to help him to salvage some of the artifacts off the *Acadia* so several of us volunteered to help. Dr. Pierce was a very interesting character and a lot of fun to work with; he was referred to by his friends as Magoo due to his extreme nearsightedness. He had been diving the *Acadia* several times previously to see how intact and exposed the wreck was and how she lay. On one of the early solo trips he said he found a ships bell and tried to bring it in but the current carried him southwest. along the shore and he got tired swimming on his back with his diving equipment and the bell on his chest and when he got into the surf it turned him over and he could find it again. He built a small barge and trailer after that, I was there for its first sea trial, we swam out to the wreck with a small line then we got to the stack then we would pull out a larger line and secure it to the stack. The others would then pull the barge with our tanks and equipment out using the rope and tie off over the wreck. Magoo was at disadvantage diving on the *Acadia* as visibility was usually measured in inches and a lot of the finds are made using the Braille system it was necessary to do everything slowly to avoid bumping into something or getting tangled in something. The only time I would move fast was when I felt a stone crab push on my hand with its pincher, there were a lot of them on the wreck but no fingers were lost. The bow of the ship is very intact and was exposed very 9 feet out of the sand, this is the last project Magoo wanted to get to the bow for the museum, it was very sharp and covered with copper sheeting up and above the water line as was the rest of the hull. He said it looked like a Viking ship. I found the pull you have in your display on the deck by the forward hold on my way to the bow. We made several dives from 1970 into 1971 when completed when I completed my diving training and left to go back to work. I think the pulley was covered in 1971. The small salvage barge Magoo made was very efficient. We would unhook the trailer then roll it into the water and launch it. The tanks and heavy equipment would ride out on it to the wreck. We would put on our equipment in the water the barge had a hole in the center that you could lower a rope thru and have two people on each side pull up heavy loads. It was easy to position over large objects. Most of the artifacts recovered were small but some were too heavy to swim up with. The stern is broken and turned at an angle to the rest of the ship and is almost entirely covered in sand. Dr. Pierce was a unique individual and I enjoyed knowing him and participating in some of his adventures.

Barry P Parks[74]

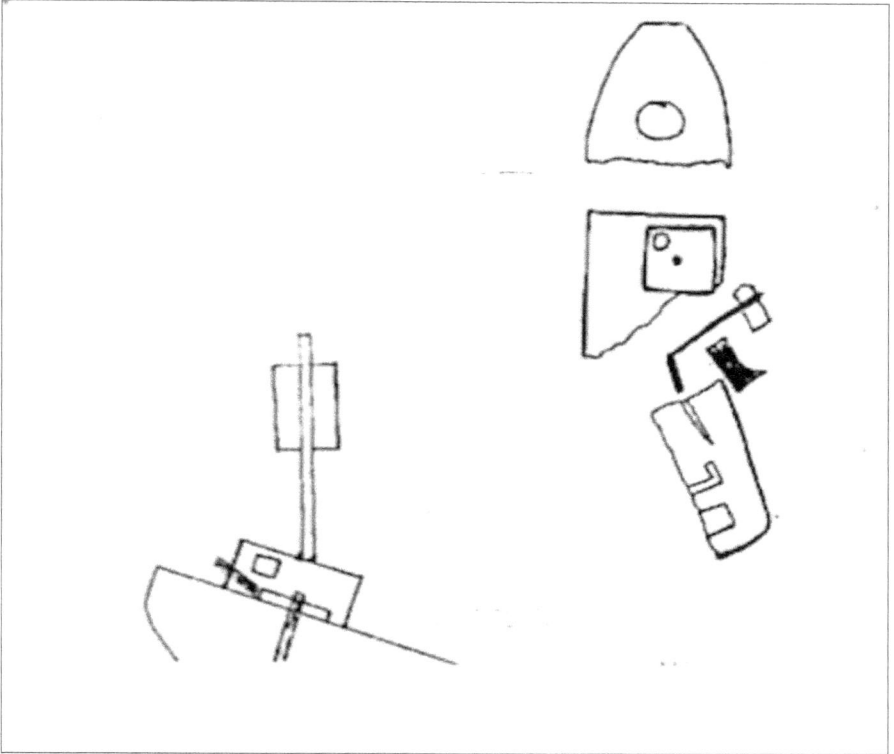

Line drawing of the *Acadia* broken apart.[75]

The Artifacts

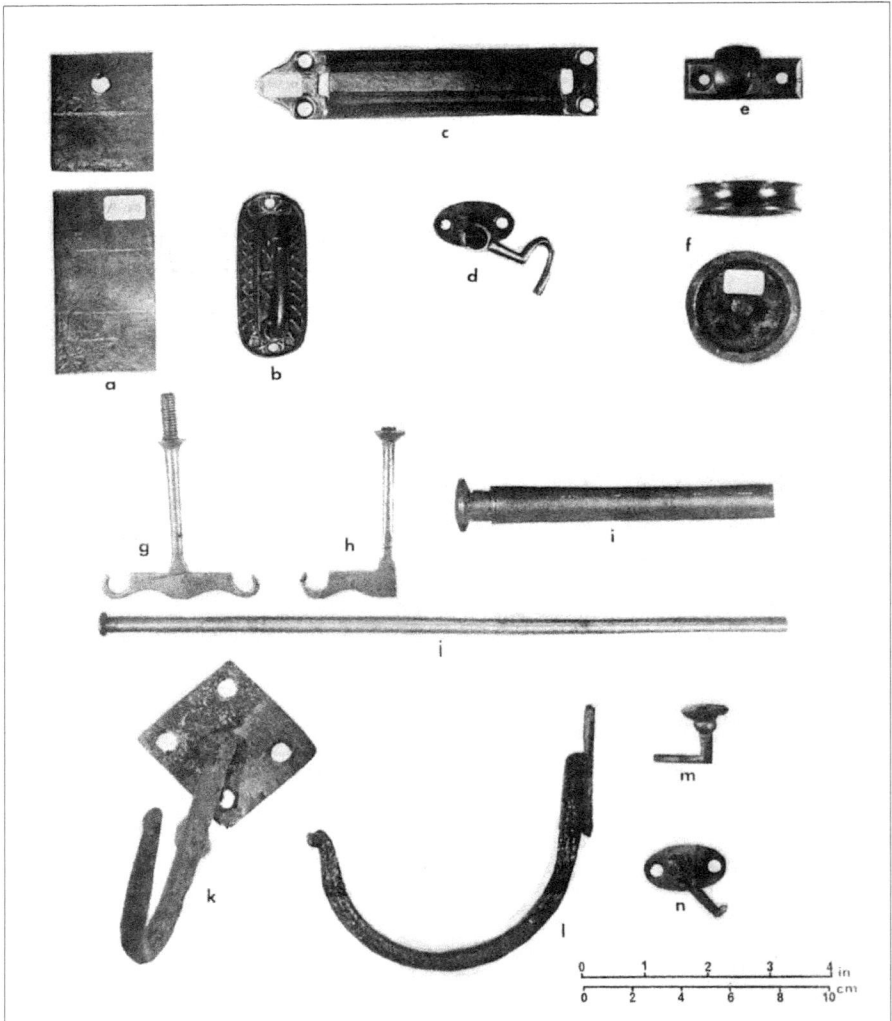

a. Brass ruler marked to inches; b. brass clothes hook; c. brass foot or chain bolt; d. n. brass cabinet hooks; e. brass sashlift; f. sash pulley, edge and plan views; g. h. vestibule hooks; i. j. vestibule rods; k. l. iron coat hooks; m. brass hook. Scale is 1:2.

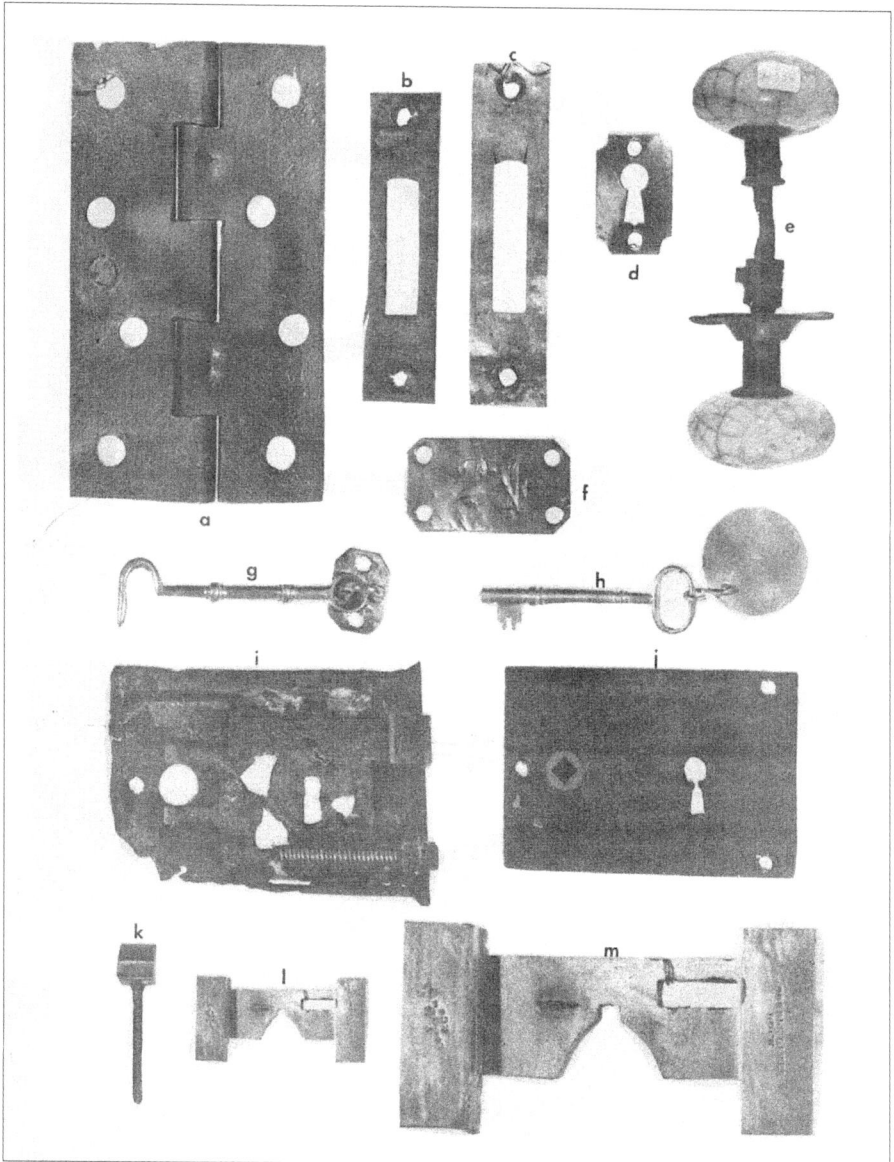

a. Brass butt hinge; b. c. brass striker plates; d. brass plated escutcheon; e. white porcelain doorknob assembly; f. brass door plate with "24" inscribed; g. brass door hook; h. brass room key with tag; i. j. inside and cover of iron door lock; k. brass door bolt with iron shaft; l. m. piece of brass double lever lock. Scale of all objects except c. m. is 1:2.

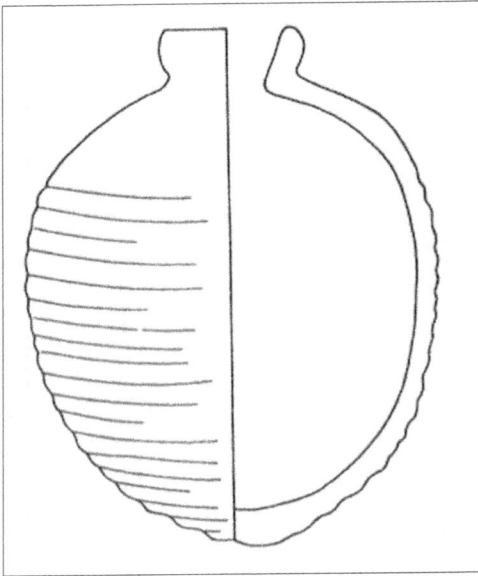

Sketches of earthenware jars recovered from the *Acadia*.

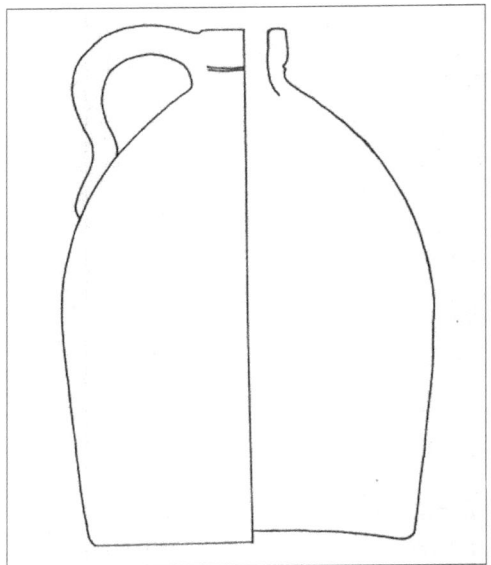

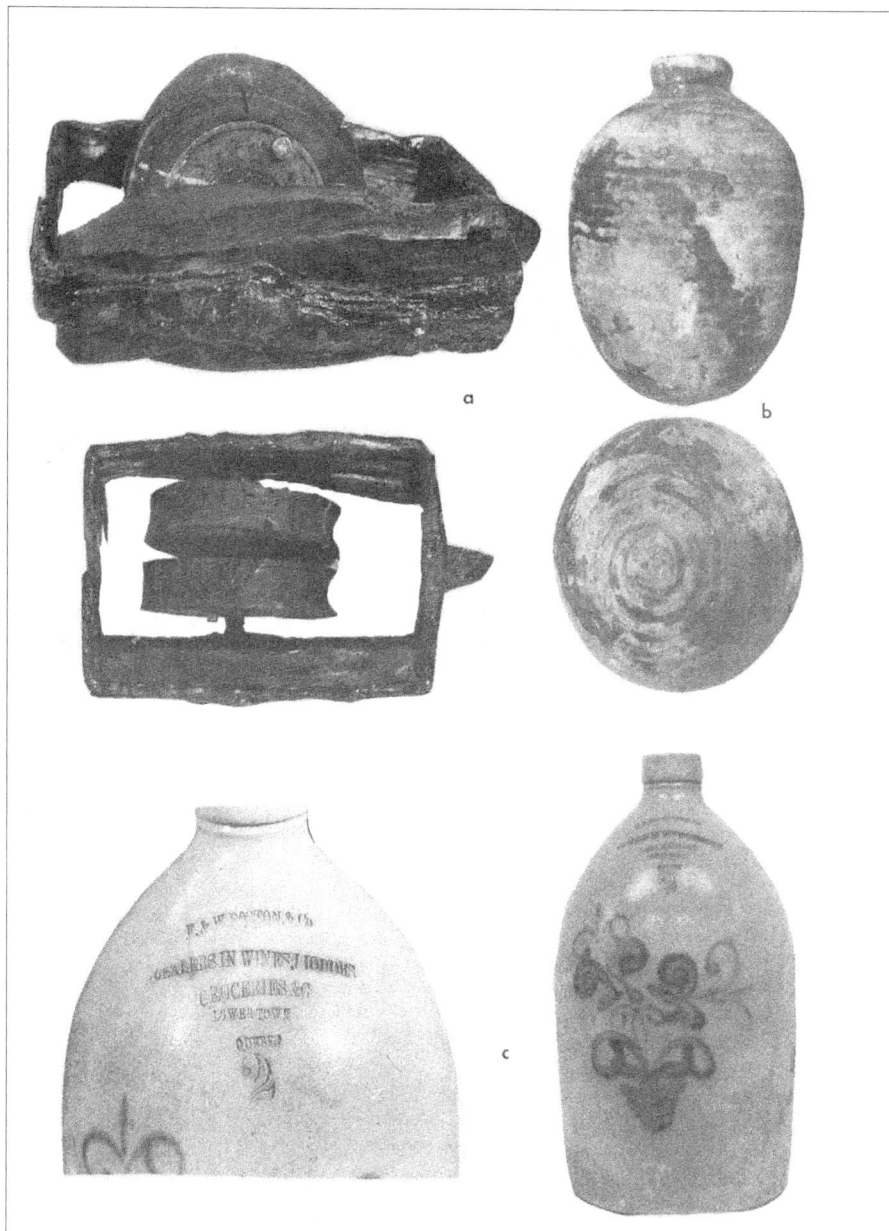

a. wood and iron block; b. earthenware olive jar; c. earthenware jug. Scale of a. b. is 1:2 and b. c. 1:4.

a. base of lead and copper sheathed bowl; b. flap valve showing soldered adjusting screws; c. lead base and valve; d. lead sheathed porcelain bowl; e. flush handle and socket; f. lead weight. Scale of components except b. about 1:10.

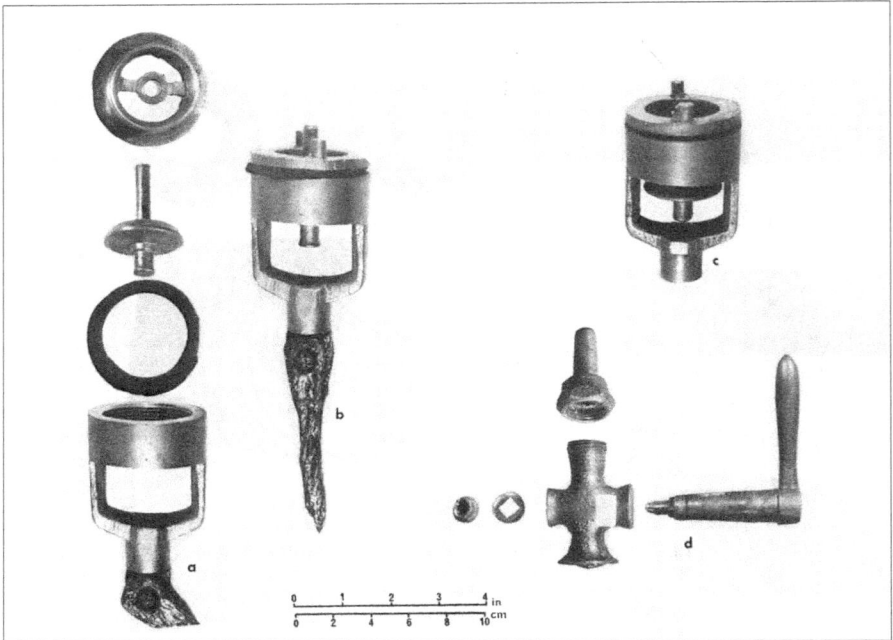

a. A. popper valve disassembled; b. c. popper valves; d. brass valve disassembled. Scale 1:2.

a. Copper overflow basins with lead pipes; b. roll of lead sheathing. Scale about 1:4.

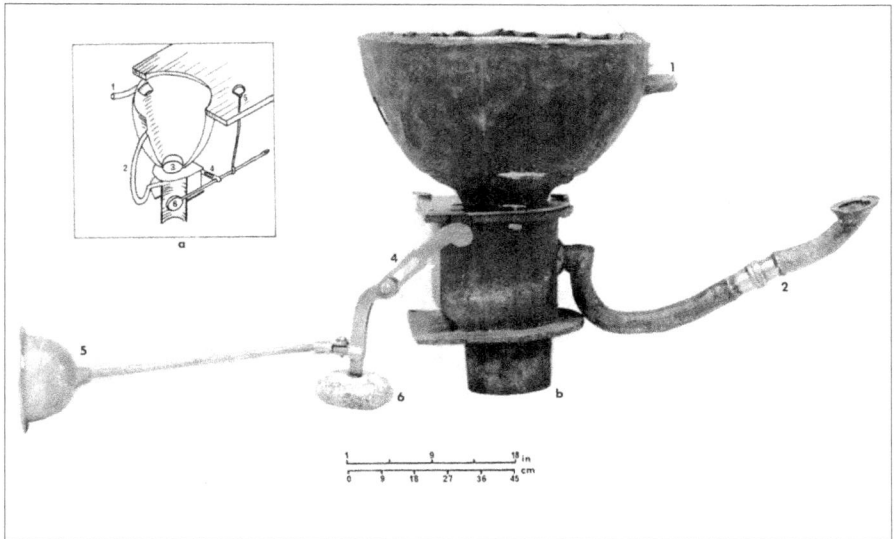

a. Cutaway reconstruction of toilet; b. toilet from *Acadia* assembled. Numbers refer to component parts: 1. Water supply; 2. Trapped overflow; 3. Flap valve; 4.operating lever; 5. Flush handle; 6. Lead weight. Scale of b is about 1:9.

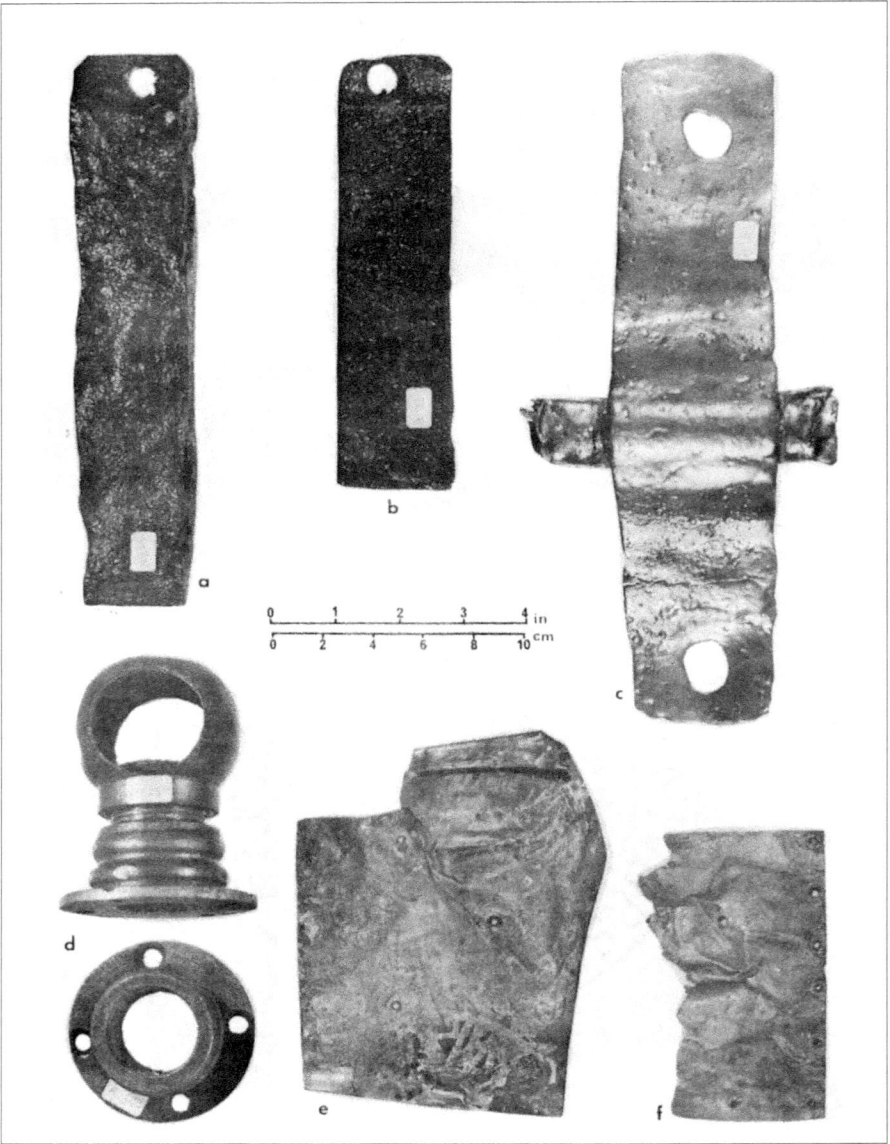

a. b. irons sash weights; c. copper pipe with mounting strap; brass railing fitting; e. f. pieces of brass sheathing. All objects 1:2.

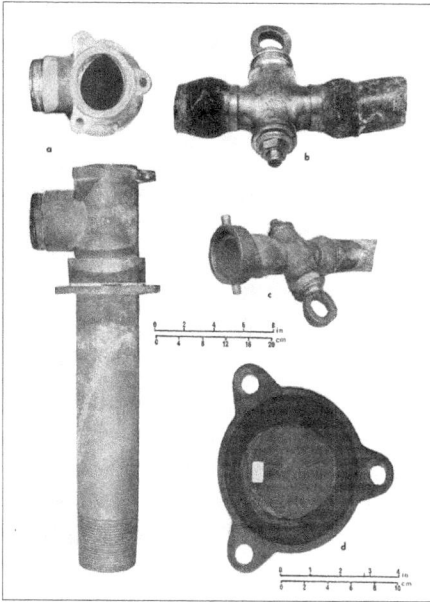

a. Brass standpipe; b. c. brass cut-off valves; d. cover for standpipe. Scale a. b. & c. 1:4; d is 1:2.

a. Bricks with iron spike attached; b. brick with motar; c. brick with wood fragments; d. brass cutoff valve with lead pipe attached; e. t-junction of lead pipe. Scale about 1:4.

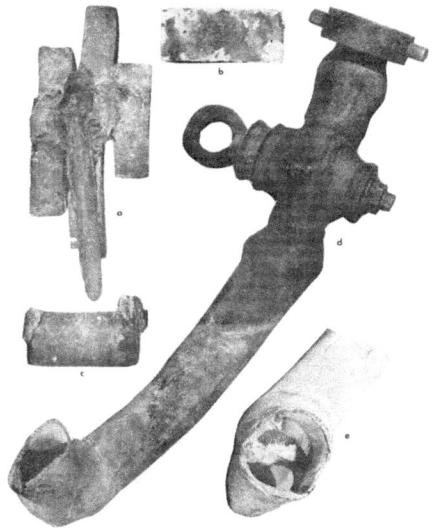

Figure 13. a, bricks with iron spike attached; b, brick with mortar; c, brick with wood fragments; d, brass cutoff valve with lead pipe attached; e, T-junction of lead pipe. Scale of a-c is 1:2; d,e, about 1:4.

Acadia

The Following Includes Pages 8 through 24

Dr. Frank Hole

Antiquities Committee[76]

Captain Leach and his crew were taken in a very friendly manner and having plenty of money made it back to Canada okay and probably lionized for their heroic deed. However, the explanation given by Leach to the ship's owners no doubt were looked at through jaundiced eye.

The *ACADIA* was exposed for the most part from the deck up, so after the war, civilians started to take her lumber and anything else they could without getting wet. As time went on the beach eroded away and year by year the *ACADIA* became further off the shore making her a good fishing spot as long as she could be waded out to. Then she could be approached by small boats. Finally after so much abuse by hurricanes and people the water covered most all of her except the miss-named structure called the "stack," which protruded ten feet above the surface today this actually was a look-out stand and boom erected above the wheel-house.

The beach had now eroded much more than a cables length too over three hundred yards from her over-picked bones, and she lies beyond the third sandbar in fifteen feet of water at normal tide lever. The wreck is very difficult to approach through the surf and strong lateral currents, even with a surfboard. Certainly, by now she should be entitled to some privacy. But no, along comes a self-styled marine archaeologist skin diving dentist to scour and rid her innards of any residual that could genuinely identify her as the Sidewheel Steamer and blockade inner.

Miraculously, the *ACADIA* is still in the identical position and place as she was on that fateful day of February 6, 1865, adhered to the clay in a vices-like grip. Her stem is majestically erect with over one hundred eighty feet of her structure intact as a physical tribute to her magnificent heritage. This fact alone should justify my tendency to exaggerate her qualities.

For generations, the local residents have known the

wreck as the "Boilers." That they were the remains of the Confederate ship that was run aground by a United States ship during the Civil War. Also, that the Confederate ship was bringing supplies to the area and the Captain and crew saved. Title or nothing else is known. In 1968, a group of local citizens erected a marker of the site commemorating rating the event. The inscriptions upon it are incorrect.

In July 1971, after preliminary diving exploration, I believe that extensive underwater investigation and historical research of the stricken vessel should be made. I then consulted Dr. T.E. Pulley, the Director of the Houston Museum of Natural Science, and received his complete approval and co-operation. All artifacts recovered were to be housed and be responsible for the Houston Museum of Natural Science. The ultimate goal was to see a display in the newly constructed Hall of Texas History, representing Naval operations of the American Civil War on our Texas shore.

In compliance with the Texas Antiquities Code, a permit was requested for and received by the Houston Museum of Natural Science, from the Texas Antiquities Committee, to investigate and recover a representative of artifacts from pre-20th- century wreck *ACADIA*.

Diving and recovery procedures were established and executed in due form.

Artifacts were treated for preservation and housed in the museum as planned.

Dr. Frank Hole, Department of Anthropology and Archeology, Rice University, is to write the official publication for the Archives of the State of Texas and shall serve as the legal adoption papers of another heroine of Texas History.

Antiquities Committee

Truett Lattimer, Chairman or Executive Secretary

Dr. T.E. Pulley, Director of the Houston Museum of Natural Science

Dr. Frank Hole, Department of Anthropology and Archeology, Rice University

At the time the *ACADIA* went aground there were
other blockade-runners in the vicinity. Two of these, the
Wren and the *Will-o' the Wisp*, were shelled and the latter
destroyed. The *Galveston Tri-Weekly News* of February 8
also mentions that sixteen blockading vessels were outside
the harbor. The sale of material from the *Will-o' the Wisp* is
recorded in the *Galveston Daily News* of February 24.[77]

II. THE ARTIFACTS

Processing

Most the artifacts recovered by Dr. Pierce we're turned
over to Dr. Pulley at the Houston Museum, but before
this was done, Pierce had cleaned many of them for display. Pierce apparently broke apart the items which were
heavily encased in rusted iron and calcium carbonate con-
cretions. In so doing he probably lost a good many Iron
objects although the brass was unaffected by his severe
treatment, He reports that he washed objects to remove
the chlorides and it is evident that he dipped most of them
in a heavy wax. He also cleaned some with an acid whose
effect is seen on the lantern. Furthermore, he attempted to
reconstruct some of the doorknobs by filling their sockets
with a pink dental cement.

When I received the material, many brass objects had
been mounted on a board cover with blue velvet. The remainder were stored in boxes in much the condition that
they were in when Pierce recovered them. I took all of the
brass objects and some of the iron to my laboratory where
I had a student process them mechanically and by electrolysis. In view of the length of time that cleaning requires, I
did not deem it practical to clean all of the objects, especially does sash weights. The cleaning proceeded throughout
1972 – 73, part of the time while I was out of the country.

Most of the artifacts are now in a stable condition even
though not all have been cleaned. Many of the brass vestibule rod and pipe fittings have been left as they were,
with an oxidation layer. With the exception of the sash
weights, most of the iron objects have been cleaned either

by electrolysis are wire brushing to remove the loose scale and rust metal. Only a few of the sections were so treated, however, and the remainder will continue to corrode. Iron objects which I cleaned are treated in a few cases where a clear plastic spray and in others with WD-40, a petroleum distillate which will prevent further rusting. The brass objects which are polished have in some instances cleaned with Brasso but most have been only wire brushed. Dr. Pierce coated many of the brass objects with a layer which has not been removed.

Description of Artifacts

Since Pierce's Notes are incomplete and it cannot be determined where many of the objects were found on the boat, it seems best simply to inventory them and to provide verbal and photographic descriptions. It is evident, however, that the artifacts came basically from two sources, the "mates storeroom" and from the fitting of the ship itself. Had Pierce have a plan of a similar vessel when he recovered the objects, it would have been a great help. Most of the objects reportedly came from the vicinity the port bow, call from the "mate's storeroom." Many of the objects from this locale were contained in an incrustation of the material in the form of a crate which Pierced reports weighed about 350 pounds. We had nowhere near 350 pounds objects remaining if we except lead pipes at brass fittings of the ship's machinery.

Objects from the area of the "Mate's" Cabin

Most of the cargo was salvaged and sold at the time of the wreck, as reported in the *Galveston Weekly News* of 22 February 1865 (Appendix 8). The material of the type recovered by Pierce does not appear in sale inventory; apparently, the bulk of the cargo was cloth and miscellaneous utilitarian objects of metal.

Pierce reports that on ships of this type, a mate's storeroom served to keep material that might be needed to in the repair a ship. He also reports that he recovered many of the objects in a chest–sized cluster weighing some 350 pounds. The objects reported from this locale look like the fittings for a wealthy person's house, although they may have served equally on board a well–fitted ship.

Pierce's Notes do not permit a precise location of the storeroom, but from the fact that the two commodes were recovered. I surmise that he was working in the area of the cabin, toilet, and locker just forward of the report paddle-wheel. The plan of the Fergus (Fig 14) shows two cabins and two commodes in this location and an adjacent locker from which some of the objects may have been taken.

As I reconstruct the situation, Pierce probably recovered a crate of "household" fittings and also the fittings of one or more of the cabins and the toilet.

Pulleys, window sash, brass (Figure 1): there are eighteen of these sash sockets, each of which consists of a circular brass casting. 1.9 to 2.0" (4.8 to 4.9 centimeters) in outer diameter, which forms the outside of the pulley. The pulley groove is .4 "(1.1 cm) between the outer edges and is .12" (.3 cm) deep. Thus, the pulley would be suitable for a quarter inch sash cord. The interior on the casting it is rough and has a central encircling groove into which an iron disc with its axle was fitted, sometimes with the aid of lead. The axle is about .8"(2.1cm) long and it is and an integral part of the disc. In some, if not all instances, this iron part of the pulley was electroplated.

Sash-weights, Iron(figure 11 a,b): Pierce removed 42 Iron sash-weights of two sizes: 14 are 9.9 x 1.8 x 1.0" (25 x 4.5 x 2.5cm); and 28 are 6.9 x 1.8 x 1.2" (17.5 x 4.5 x 3 cm). Each weight of cast-iron has a hole in its upper end. The holes," about .5" (1.2 cm) in diameter, held this sash cords. These objects were heavily corroded and only a few have been given electrolytic processing. After our processing, the most nearly intact small example weighs 1342 grams (a little over 3 pounds), and the largest one is 1495 grams (about 3 1/4 pounds); much of the material has corroded from the latter example.

Sash lifts, brass (Figure 1 e): there are two sash lifts each which was cast as a single unit consisting of a rectangular plate and a broad curve hook. Each plate has two countersunk screw holes and has beveled edges.

Vestibule rods, brass (Figure 1f.j): The 22 rods are clearly designed to fit inside the rod hangers. Each rod consists of a tubular piece of brass, 22.8" (57.8) long and .6" (1.57 cm) in an outside diameter. The rods are about .05"(.15 cm) thick and are welded or brazed to form the tube. In one end of this tube, a cast brass fitting was inserted to fit into hooks on the rod hangers (Fig 1 i). Each two is only one and with this fitting so that the rods were evidently used in pairs. The means by which the two sections were joined is not known. Modern rods at this time are made up to diameters so that one can slip over the other.

Vestibule rod hangers, brass (Fig 1 g.h): two styles are represented, T-Shaped and L-shaped. The hangers are all cast of brass. There are three sides of the T-shaped variety: 6.7 x 5.0 (17.1 x 12.7 cm)' 2) 7.0 x 5.0 or 4.8" (17.7 x 12.7 or 12.3 cm); and 3) 7.1 x 5.1" (18.0 x 13.0 cm)/ The two L-shaped hangers are 5.1 x 2.8 (13.0 x 7.2 cm) and 5.2 x 2.8" (13.1 x 7.2 cm) respectively.

The T – shaped hangers have a flange which, in most instances, was cast as part of the peace and in two examples as a separate peace which was joined (whether it is socketed into the hanger or forced over a rod is not certain). Below the flange is a bolt, the best example of which has 12 threads to the inch (Figure 1 g). In all cases, the end of the bolt casting has a slight depression which was made when the bolts were turned on the lathe. The opposite (T-end) and of the peace has a similar indentation.

The L– shaped variety is one half of a T – shaped hanger, on which one arm of the T was not cast. The L – shaped hangers were mounted differently too; both examples have a distal flange slipped over an inner core and to this flange, a rectangular brass plate is riveted (Figure 1 h). The play is four corner holes for attaching to the ceiling.

The hangers of both styles were probably made to hold the clothes rods in the wardroom. The T – shaped were used where there was more room, whereas the L – shaped variety could be placed directly against a wall. The worn bolts on most of the examples indicate that they had been used.

Clothes hooks, Iron (Figure 1 k.l.): Two books have brass place with a stamp design, X's around the edge and a floral design in the center. The hooks are riveted on with washers on the underside of the plates.

Coat hooks, Iron (Figure 1b): The seven iron hooks are you nearly identical. They consist of a square plate about 2 x 2" (5 x 5 cm) to which a curved hook was riveted. Both hooks and plates appear to have been forged. Each plate has 4 screw holes in its corners.

Doorknobs, White porcelain (Figure 2 e): the pieces suggest that doorknobs we're sent as complete units comprising two knobs, a brass flange, and a square–sectioned iron connecting rod. The activating mechanism is a two–armed brass lever which was forged on to that center of the iron connecting rod. Of the 14 knobs, however only five are parts of intact units; on one of these one knob is missing. The remaining knobs consist only the knob itself and then brass shaft and, in some instances, the brass flange.

The knobs average about 2.2' (5.6 cm) in diameter. There is somewhat more variability in their brass shafts which range from .7 to 1.1' (1.8 to 2.7 cm) in length and from .5 to .6' (1.3 to 1.6 cm) in diameter. Some of these shafts are flared at the distal end. In the complete units, the shaft with the flared end is opposite the knob with the flange. In other words, the flared shaft was designed to fit directly against the door, whereas on the other side (inside) the flange served this purpose. Thus five of the 14 knobs go on the inside of the door.

The shafts have two sizes of screws or pinholes Typically one of each pair is about .1" (.3cm) in diameter whereas the other is somewhat elliptical and about .2" (.6 cm) in diameter. In examples where it can be seen, iron pins or screws were used; there are no screw threads on the examples where the pin is not present. The flange has two holes about .2" (.6 cm) in diameter for screws. One example shows that when the brass shots did not seat tightly into the knob, they were filled with molten lead.

Doorknobs, brown ambled "Mineral": Four examples of knobs, none of which is attached to a complete unit, were preserved. Like the white examples, these were apparently fired onto the shafts. However, all the shafts were of iron and three of the examples were leaded into place.

The broken example shows, however, that the intent was to fire the units together without the necessity for leading. The lack of connecting rods is probably due to the fact that the hardware for the knobs was made entirely of iron.

Drawer pulls, white porcelain: Two examples are in the collection. They are about 1.3" (3.3cm) in diameter and were fired as a unit with a porcelain shaft. To this shaft, we added a brass flange. The surviving flange is embossed with two concentric rings of punctuation's and has a hole punched in the edge for a nail or screw. The inside of the pull has a rectangular hole .2" (.6 cm) on a side which would slip over an iron connection rod if it had been mounted for that purpose. On the drawer pull, however, the hole is flush with the shaft and would not have slipped over a rod.

Parts of the locks, brass, and iron (Figure 2 k-m): Two brass lock bolts with iron drive shafts, one of which retains a brass spring and the U-shaped bracket which works against the turning lever of the doorknob assembly. In both instances, the shafts were screwed into the bracket so the distance could be adjusted.

Another item is a piece of a brass "double lever lock", according to the message stamped on one side. This piece also has a trademark, of "Y & Co" and a key, stamped on it (Figure 2 1.m)

Lock, iron (Figure 2 i,j): One iron door lock is nearly intact. It consists of a rectangular, two-piece box, whose cover is 4.7 x 3.2" (12 x 8 cm). On the cover is a company name which is partially obliterated. According to correspondence between Dr. Pierce and the Sergeant & Company of New Haven, the lock was manufactured by Davenport & Mallory. With this clue, the name DM & Co, NEW HAVEN can be made out on the lock. A similar lock was apparently sent to the company by Pierce and is now in the collection of the New Haven Historical Society.

The lock incorporates the doorknob mechanism as well as a key bolt. The doorknob bolt is similar to the ones that go with the doorknobs except that the mounting bracket is of offset to allow space for the key. The key bolt is a simple spring-loaded device of a kind which would be turned by the keys in the collection. The striker plates in the collection are too small to have been used with this size lock.

In his notes, Pierce says that the "D.M. & Co. NEW HAVEN" was inscribed on the back of several door locks of ferrous metal. They were in surprisingly good condition, aside from the one he sent to New Haven, and the one in the present collection, the whereabouts of the others is unknown. In his correspondence with the lock company, Pierce says that one lock was found with its knob in place.

Escutcheon plates, brass plated (Figure 2 d): The five items in the group were stamped by the same die from stock .05" (.12 cm) thick. One example appears, from the scoring around the screw hole, to have been used. The screw holes are all beveled from the outer face and appear to have been punched out. The diameter of the holes is .2" (.5 cm); the keyhole is .9" (2.2 cm) long. The metal stock is not rusted and is the color of tin. A thin brass plating was applied to both sides of the stock.

Striker plates, brass (Figure 2 b,c): Twenty-two of these pieces of hardware were recovered. These were cut rather than stamped from sheets of brass,03" (.8 cm) thick. Apparently, three steps comprised the making of these pieces. First, the sheets were cut into rectangles of 1.2 x 4.9" (3 x 12.4 cm). Evidence of the cutting blades is seen on some examples whose edges were cut into accidentally (Figure 2 b). It is probable that several plates were cut at one time and that occasionally one in the stack slipped as it was being turned on the cutting table. Second, the rectangular cutout was made. The cutout is .5 x 2.1" (1.3 by 5.4 cm) and is rectangular except for one slightly rounded end. Cut marks on all examples at the rounded end are evident of the way these holes were made. It is likely that a three-sided die on a rocker lever was used. Thus the rectangular portion of the hole was cut, leaving one end uncut and leaving two grooves from the sides of the die impressed in the place (Figure 2 cm). The next step would be to cut the rounded end, probably with a hand-held chisels-like die. This cut would truncate the grooves.

The final step in making the striker plates was to punch screw holes. This was done to stack the plates simultaneously, as indicated by the fact that several plates are still stuck together by the punched holes. One such stack includes seven plates. Scoring around the holes on a few plates suggests use but equally, it may have resulted from twisting and turning the punch as the holes were made.

One plate's holes are torn out and another retains a portion of a metal plate which is probably part of the lock in a door. Thus, some of striker plates may have been in bundles for sale and others may have been part of the ship's fittings.

Keys, brass (Figure 2 h): Six keys remain in the collection; to three of these there are round brass plates with identifying letters attached by brass S-shaped hooks. Each of the keys fits s different lock. Five examples are of the same type and fit simple pin tumblers, but the one labeled N fits a tumbler with horizontal pins.

Butt hinges, brass (figure 2 a): Twenty-nine hinges of four sizes are in the collection. The hinges are all cast butt hinges with four nail/screw holes in each half. Iron pins remain in most of the specimens. The dimensions of the four groups are: 1) 3.75 x 2.2 x.1" (9.5 x 5.6 x .3 cm) 2) 3.5 x 2.0 x 1" (9.0 x 5.2 x .25 cm) 3) 3.5 x 1.9 x .1" (8.9 x 4.8 x .2 cm); and 4) 3.3 x1.9 x .1" (8.3 x 5.0 x .2 cm) A screw hole in one hinge is ripped out but this may have resulted from the shelling of the boat; otherwise the hinges appear to have been unused and were probably part of the cargo for sale.

Foot or chain bolt, brass (Figure 1 c): Part of a foot or chain bolt, consisting of a cast brass receptacle for a bolt remains, but the strike plate is missing. This device would have received a bolt no larger than .4 x 2" (1 x .5 cm). The receptacle is 3.7" (9.3 cm) long and the outside dimensions are 5.5 x 1.1" (14 x 2.9 cm): It was attached by means of nails and screws inserted through four holes which were punched or drilled through the piece. The piece is about .1" (.25 cm) thick.

Hooks, brass (Figure 1 d, n; 2 g): There are two door hooks, each with its brass attachment plate. Each is about 3.9" (10 cm) long and is attached to its plate with a U-ring which is riveted to the plate (Figure 2 g).

There are also three cabinet hooks, one of which is broken (Figure 1 n). They are about 1.7" (4.2 cm) long and are attached to the plate by a split ring which has been closed and forced into a rectangular hole in the plate.

Hurricane lamp, brass, and glass (Figure 3 f): "One lantern, intact enough for reconstruction, is in the collection. The pieces remaining are the glass globe, the base, three of the vertical brass wine bails, both horizontal bails, and the ring top to which the bails were attached by riveting and soldering. Since there is no evidence of a wick holder, kerosene reservoir or top, this may have been a candle lamp. The lantern originally had six vertical and two horizontal bails. Aside from a nick in the base of the globe the glass is in excellent condition. The globe appears to have been blown and had encircling bands applied to the top and bottom. The joining of the ends of the upper bands is especially apparent.

The base is of two pieces, the ring base stand which is perforated for ventilation, and a horizontal flange ring which has been perforated to receive the lower ends of the vertical bails. This flange ring is soldered to the ring base.

Earthenware jar (Figure 4, 5 C): Pierce does not state where he found the perfectly preserved earthenware jug with the stamped message

F. & P. Poston. & Co. (sic) E&W Poston and Co.
DEALERS IN WINE, LIQUORS
GROCERIES & C
LOHERTOHN
QUEBEC

John Howells told me that another diver recovered it from the ship. The jar has a salt glaze on the outside and a brown glaze on the inside. The lettering and a large floral pattern in blue were applied before the glaze. The jar is 14.6" (37 cm) high with a maximum diameter of 9.9" (25 cm). It has a simple strap handle.

Note:
John Howells was a past President of the Houston Civil War Roundtable and a good friend of Dr. Pierce. It was a

Civil War Historical Society. Bob Windsor worked for Tenneco, later he worked for Trammel Crow in Dallas.

The earthenware jug was found with another earthenware jug inside an encrusted crate that was brought up from the *Acadia*. It was part of the cargo. When we pulled up the crates, that is when Officer Paige blocked the traffic for us to pull the crates from the water to Dr. Pierce's car to take back to Dr. Frank Hole at Rice University for restoration and cataloging.[78]

Earthenware jar (Figure 4, 5 C): Pierce does not state where he found the perfectly preserved earthenware jug with the stamped message

F. & P. Poston. & Co. (sic) E&W Poston and Co.
DEALERS IN WINE, LIQUORS
GROCERIES & C
LOHERTOHN
QUEBEC

Olive jars (Figure 5 b, 6): There are three earthenware olive jars in the collection. They are all of the same size, 11.6" (29.5 cm) high with maximum diameter of about 9" (23 cm). The necks have an OD of 3.5" (8,5 cm) and an ID of 1.6" (4 cm). The jars show coiling at the base (Figure 5 b) and up the entire body and have glaze inside and out. A shard of another olive jar is also in the collection.

Fragment of wood: A piece of wood 1.8 x 6.7 x1.0" (4.5 x 17 x 2.5 cm) has two nail holes in it with an impression of a metal strap. The end of the piece shows tongue and groove joining. Thus, the piece may have been the reinforced corner of a window frame, door, or chest.

Piece of glass: A piece of hand-blown dark green colored glass with numerous air bubbles is in the collection.

Ruler, brass (Figure 1 a): Two pieces of a brass ruler marked in inches were recovered. The longer segment has inches 3, 4 and 5, whereas the smaller portion is marked with 21 and 22. The latter section also has a hole in its ends suggesting it was either mounted or hung. The numbers punched into its face, and the lines were cut with a chisel-like punch. The ruler is made of a sheet of brass .03" (.1 cm) thick and is 1.6" (4 cm) wide.

Hook, brass (Figure 1m): A hook cast as one piece consists of right-angle hook, rounded in section, .2" (.45 cm) in diameter, with a basal flange oval in plan with a maximum dimension of .8" (1.95 cm). The flange has a hole in its bottom which may have been attached to a bolt or rivet.

Door plate, brass (Figure 2 f): This piece is a rectangular plate with the number 24 punched and/or scored into its surface. The number is made up of a series of lines and with some decorative, linear infilling. The dimensions are 2.8 x 1.5" (7 x 3.8 cm) and the corners are cut off. At each corner is a nail/screw hole. The plate is .04" (.09 cm) thick.

Brass disc: According to Pierce, "Another trade mark was Unicorn and Lion with 'J.M. Carpenter' patents on a piece of brass the size of a twenty-five cent. coin. Whatever it had been attached to was destroyed." This piece is not in the present collection.

Flush toilet (Figure 7,8): Although Pierce extolled to find the toilet and asserted that it was the one that made Thomas Crapper famous, he was incorrect. According to the biography of Crapper, which Pierce cites, Crapper opened his plumbing show only in 1861 after having worked as an apprentice plumber since 1848. The cistern for which he became famous was patented sometime after 1872. The model toilet, which was fitted into the Acadia, must have been produced within a year or so of the time when he went into business in competition with many other manufacturers. In fact, its design goes back to 1770 and is known as "Bramah's closet."

The toilet is a remarkable object however whose recovery was effected under the most difficult of circumstances. Pierce walked to shore with the device, after having discarded his breathing tanks. Every so often he kicked to the surface for a breath of air and then settled back to the bottom to plod forward.

The device is relatively simple, consisting of a bowl sheathed in lead, a brass flush valve, and activator mechanism. With this kind of device, it was necessary to turn the water on separately, it would seem, for it was Crapper himself who invented the flush device that we know today.

When I received the toilet it had been assembled after

having been taken apart by Pierce for cleaning. Thus, the exact relationship of the parts remains somewhat uncertain. Nevertheless, with some confidence, we can reconstruct the toilet as is shown in Figure 7a. In this reconstruction, a wooden seat has been added. It will be seen that the activating handle is set in a brass bowl in the seat itself. This reconstruction is redrawn from a similar device illustrated in *A History of Technology* vol. 4, Fig. 285 (1958).

The mechanism of the commode is interesting and deserves an extended description. It comprises a base cast in lead, which serves to anchor the commode to its wooden framework and also to seat the bowl, the flush valve, and the lower water inlet (Figure 8 c). Overall this component is 11" (23 cm) high. The lower outlet has an OD of 4: (10.0 cm) and an ID of 3.3" (8.5 cm). At 2.6" (6.5 cm) up from the base is a mounting flange which is 8.7" x 7.4" (22 x 18.8 cm). In this flange are three holes for bolts. The upper flange is 7.5" x 6.3" (19 x 16 cm) and has five bolt holes.

On top of this flange, the flush valve sits and is attached by five brass bolts whose heads are triangular in shape (Figure 8c). The valve mechanism is solid brass comprising an activating lever and the valve itself, which is simple, a disc with a beveled edge, which fits into the outlet, which is correspondingly beveled. The valve has four adjusting screws to level it so that it seats tightly against the outlet (Figure 8 b). Although these screws were soldered in place, the valve is now out of adjustment and will not seat properly.

The toilet bowl slips over the upper part of the brass valve mechanism. It consists of a porcelain bowl, which is entirely clad in a sheath of lead (Figure 8 d). The lower 2.4" (6 cm) of the lead sheath is further clad in a copper sheath (Figure 8 a). The bowl and valves were probably leaded together when the commode was ready for use. The bowl has an OD of 13.5" (35 cm) and an ID of 11.2" (28.5 cm). The porcelain bowl has a flat-topped rim projecting at right angles inward about 1.4" (6 cm). Overall the bowl is 8.5" (21.5 cm) high.

The inlet to the bowl consists of a lead pipe, which enters near the top of the bowl. Splashing is reduced by a lead flap, which hangs down over the inlet and directs the waste downward. This pipe and flap are mounted to the bowl with brass bolts.

The other parts of the commode are lead weight (Figure 8f) which attaches to the valve lever, and a plunger handle which activates the lever (Figure 8 e). The plunger handle fits into a brass cup, which was mounted on the toilet seat. The handle is attached to a brass tube which screws into both the handle and the fitting attached to the weight. A vertical pull on the handle would thus open the valve and the weight would keep it tightly seated when it was not in use.

Mechanically it is an awkward device if all of the component parts are present. It would appear that there is an undue amount of strain on the plunger owing to the position of the weight, which tends to pull the plunger out of the vertical plane. I assume, in consequence, that there is a piece missing.

Fragments of toilet bowl: Pierce also found six shards from the other porcelain bowl. They fit together to give a nearly to base section. Except for the base, the exterior is glazed. The base section is demarked by a horizontal encircling grooved and by an open crosshatch pattern scored into the clay.

Overflow basins, copper (figure 9 arc): Both of these objects were apparently mounted, to judge from the fact that their mounting flanges are torn where they fit wrenched free of their rivets or bolts. For this reason, it would appear that they were part of the functioning equipment and not spare parts. Pierce reports that they came from the toilet area.

It would appear that they were designed to catch overflow, which drained into the basin and exited either through the spout or down the vertical copper pipe, which is connected through a threaded brass fitting to a lead pipe. Alternatively, water flowed up into the basin and out the spout. Neither alternative makes much sense in the context of a toilet area where running water would either flow into a basin or, perhaps, from a shower. I see no way that these could have been attached to the commodes and they would not have served well as urinals, as Pierce suggested. I would guess that these objects are from the engine room which is near the cabin and toilet area.

The basins are made of copper which was formed into a rectangular shape and sealed with a white cement. Their inner dimensions are 7.2 x 4.7 x 4.7" deep (18.3 x 11.8 x 11.8 cm). The spout has an ID of 2.4" (6 cm), and the upright pipe, 2.6' (6.5cm). The latter pipe is about 15" (38 cm) long.

Short, copper tubes, brass: Three objects appear to be brass tubes to which covers were soldered. The tubes are about.03" (.1 cm) thick and are 1.9 to 2.0" (4.9 to 5 cm) long, and 1.2" (3 cm) in diameter. Each tube, which was once welded, is now either totally or partially split along the seam. Each is scored with a horizontal line a .2" (6 cm) from one end and has a hole centered on this line, drilled into it. The holes are .15" (.4 cm) in diameter. One example has a brass disc soldered inside flush with the end. Traces of solder on the other examples indicate that they too had caps. These are probably cartridge casings of about 112 caliber.

Cartridge, lead: There is also a probable cartridge, which fits into the casing described above. Although somewhat pitted and deformed, enough of the shape remains to suggest that it is a cartridge. The cartridge has a concavity to one side of the center of the base. Assuming that the holes in the cartridge are to allow the firing pin access to the fulminate, the hollow base may have held the fulminate and the powder charge may have been behind, as in the case of German small arms ammunition of the 1850s. The cartridge weighs 94 grams.

Valves, brass (Figure 10d): There are two solid brass valves, apparently for use with steam or water lines. One can be completely disassembled to reveal its component parts. It consists of a cross-shaped casting, the valve stem and handle, washer, nut, connecting nut and a short length of brass tubing.

The central casting is threaded to receive the connecting nut and tube. Its opposite end is a flange into which a tube was apparently forced; there are no threads on this end. The cross piece consists simply of a tube through which the valve stem fits. The valve stem is a tapered brass rod with a horizontal slit and a machined bolt at the end opposite the handle. The washer has a square hold which fits over a corresponding square "nut" just behind the threads to prevent its turning. The nut is flared at the proximal end and hexagonal shape on the distal end. There was probably a fiber washer inserted behind the brass washer. The brass tube is sealed with a lead washer.

The other valve is constructed differently and is probably a steam cock. It is T-shaped with the inlet at the base of the T. The inlet is flanged and threaded and has a .3" (.7 cm) diameter hold in the center. On the top of the T is a relief port (?). The exit of the valve is a .3" (.7 cm) ID threaded tube which is integral to the valve stem. It has an eccentric nut to which a similarly D-shaped washer was fitted. The retaining nut is the same as in the other example except for being larger. The valve stem, in order to transmit water/steam around a right angle, must be slit differently than in the previous example.

Object probably from other locations

Railing fittings, brass (Figure 11 d): Fittings for the handrail, probably in the forward companionway are of two varieties. There are four pipe flanges of cast brass, each with four screw holes in its base, threaded for 1 1/4 inches OD iron pipe. Which means if the pipe these were attached to cast brass railheads, consisting of hollow round fittings through which a handrail of wood 1 1/2 inches in diameter could be passed. One of these still has the original iron pipe inside. Fitted in this way these pieces held the rail out from the bulkhead about 1 1/4 inches.

The remaining example consists of the brass flange into which has been slipped a welded or brazed brass tube about .04" (.1cm) in thickness and 1.5" (3.8 cm) in diameter. The railhead has been slipped over this tube to produce a rail holder about 13.8" (35 cm) long. This piece is perfectly bent. The flanges have two sets of threads. Those, which received the connecting pipe, are 1.5' ID, whereas those at the base are 1.1/8" ID. Instead of using screws, the flanges could have been mounted on pipes.

Poppet valve, brass (Figure 10 alb, c): Two of these objects, probably from the steam engine, are in the collection.
Each consists of three separate cast elements, a base with
two projecting studs for mounting, a fiber washer, and a
threaded shaft with a beveled opening; the valve stem or
plunger which fits on a rod into the base piece and nests
into the beveled opening; the upper frame which threads
onto the base and to which is threaded anion spike, It
looks as if these valves were mounted on a steam line and
secured in place with the iron spike.

Both valves are the same size. In height, the unit is 3.4'
(8.5 cm). The valve has a diameter of 1.4" (3.5 cm). The
forged spike is split to fit over an iron pin mounted in the
top of the brass casting. The spike is now 4" (10 cm) long.

Standpipe with cap, brass (figure 12 a,d): Pierce reported finding these objects in the port bay area. They probably
came from the engine room/boiler area. The standpipe is
designed to bolt onto a deck or frame and transmit water
or steam horizontally from that point. Overall this pipe is
25.2" (64 cm) long with a flange containing four bolt holes
about two-thirds of the way up the pipe. The pipe has an
outside diameter of 4.3" (11 cm) and an ID of 3.5" (8.8 cm).
Attached just above the flange is a horizontal pipe 3.0" (7.7
cm) long, 3.5" (9 cm) OD and 2.7" (6.8 cm) ID.

The cap fits on top of the standpipe by means of three
bolts attached through perforated lugs (Figure 12 d). The
bolts are not in the collection although Pierce removed the
cap while the pipe was still attached to the ship. The cap
is solid brass 4.9" (12.5 cm) OD and .75" (1.9 cm) thick.
The inside was cut out on a lathe to a depth of .4" (1.1 cm
)to give an inner diameter of 4.4: (11.2 cm). Still inside, in
excellent pliable shape, is the rubber gasket, .5" (1.3 cm)
wide and .24" (.6 cm) thick.

Cut-off or check valve, brass, with lead pipe (Figure 12
b, c; 13 d): One example of a check valve consists of a central casting into which the valve stem is fitted, and a washer and nut assembly (Figure 12 b). The valve is operated by
means of a ring 3.5" (9 cm) in diameter with an ID of 1.6"
(4 cm). The lead pipes are slipped over the valve casting
and sealed with a large ring of lead which was hammered

over both the pipes and the valve casting. The pipe has an ID of 3.0" (7.5 cm) and is .2" (.6 cm) thick.

According to Pierce, this valve was found near the port bow where he found the brass standpipe. Although he had intended to leave this device on board so that he could secure his lines to it, treasure hunters tried to remove it thinking that it was part of a cannon. Pierce then sawed through the lead pipe and removed the object.

A second cut off valve (Figure 12 c, 13 d,e) is about the same size as the first but it includes two short segments of lead pipe, one of which is attached to a brass connector (Figure 12 c) and the other joins a transverse lead pipe. Overall the length of these fittings is 31.5" (80 cm). The OD of the horizontal valve pipe is 2.5" (6.4 cm). The brass connector at the end is 4.3" (11 cm) OD diameter and has an inner diameter of 2.28" (5.8 cm). The lead pipe is about .2" (5 cm) thick. The opposite pipe consists of two components, an interior lead pipe of 2.5" (6.4 cm) and an out sleeve which fits over its entire length. The inner pipe ends at the T-junction where the horizontal lead pipe joins (Figure 13 e) This pipe is too battered to measure accurately.

Lead pipe with brass connector (Figure):3 g,h): A length of pipe about 69" (175 cm) in length with a brass connector attached to one end. The lead pipe has an OD of 1.8" (4.5 cm) and is roughly .1" (.3 cm) thick. The connector (Figure 3 h) has an OD of 2.2" (5.5 cm) and an ID of 1.4" (3.5 cm). The opposite end of the lead pipe has been broken off.

Pipe with mounting strap, copper (Figure 11 c): This is a short segment of copper tubing about 2.8 cm in diameter and 4.7" (12 cm) long with a thickness of .4" (.1 cm). The mounting strap is roughly 2.4" (6 cm) wide and 11.8" (30 cm) long, of a thickness of .06" (.15 cm). Each end of the strap is perforated with a roughly oval hole about .78" (2 cm) in the long dimension. The strap is soldered to the pipe.

Copper or brass sheathing (figure 11 e,f): A number of pieces of the sheathing that covered the hull were removed by Dr. Pierce. Most of these are fragmentary. The large piece in the collection is evidently cut from a still larger piece as there are no nail holes in it. This sheet presently measures about 17.7 x 16.5″ (45 x 42 cm) although there is a rectangular piece cleanly cut from this area. The sheet is .2″ (.05 cm) thick.

The other pieces of sheathing are smaller, torn and worn through in places. These pieces clearly show that nails were spaced about 3-inch intervals along the edge and were sometimes placed in the body of the sheet as well. Sheathing was originally made in pieces about 2 by 4 feet.

<u>Strips of lead sheathing (Figure 9 b)</u>: A rolled bundle of three strips of lead, probably removed from the stern, which Dr. Pierce said was covered with this material, are in the collection. The strips are about 5.5″ (14 cm) wide at one end and taper to a point at the other. Overall, the bundle as now constituted, is 13.8 x 8.3 x 7″ (35 x 21 x 17 cm). The strips have nail holes in them.

<u>Coal:</u> One rounded lump of coal, 10.6 x 5.9 x 7.5″ (27 x 15 x 19 cm) in the only piece of this material recovered by Pierce. He mentions that there are many more.

<u>Pipe, lead (Figure 3 a)</u>: A segment of lead pipe about 7.1″ (18 cm) long, with OD of about 1.1″ (2.7 cm). One end is flared to fit onto another pipe or fitting. The pipe is approximately .15″ (.4 cm) thick.

A section of lead pipe, flared at both ends is about 12.2″ (31 cm) long, with OD of 1.6″ (4 cm) and is about .2″ (.5 cm) thick (Figure 3 a). Both flared ends have nail holes in them.

<u>Connector, brass:</u> Probably a connector for a steam pipe, this piece is made from a single casting. It consisted of a connecting element 2″ (5 cm) long and a flattened tang which was riveted with three brass rivets to another object. The tang is also perforated with a nail/screw hole. The connector is perforated at the tang and with a .4″ (.9 cm) diameter hole which extends 1.3″ (3.2 cm) into the connector. The opposite end is threaded. Its ID is .78″ (2.0 cm).

<u>Tube, copper (Figure 3 c)</u>: A length of copper tube about 4.1″ (10.5 cm) long with an OD of roughly .4″ (.9 cm). The tube walls are about .04″ (.1 cm) thick. The tube appears

to be seamless.

Wire, copper (Figure 3 b): Two short lengths of copper wire, .08 (.2 cm) in diameter.

Disc, iron with washer: A disc, 1.7" (4.3 cm) in diameter, .5" (1.2 cm) thick, with a fiber washer attached by means of a forged rivet, is in the collection. The disc is roughly shaped by filing.

Nails, brass (Figure 3 e): There are two cast nails whose shanks have been mannered into roughly a rectangular section. The heads are both askew suggesting that the nails had been driven into wood. Each is 1.1" (2.8 cm) long and fits well in the holes in various pieces of hardware. Pierce reports recovering nails from the hull sheathing.

Screw, brass (Figure 3 d)" The screw has a head diameter of 1/4 inch and is 3/4 inch long (.7 x 1.9 cm) There are seven threads in the half-inch of the shank.

Fiber gasket: A gasket about .7" (1.7 cm) in diameter with a hole about .24" (.6 cm) in diameter probably was attached to one of the valves.

Eye, of iron?" A fragment of a larger piece. All the remains in the eye, about .2" (.4 cm) in diameter.

Bricks (Figure 13 a-c): In digging about the boiler, Pierce found numerous firebricks. He notes the presence of "reinforcement metal that was constructed inside of the bricks were made. This was necessary to hold the bricks together with the help of the mortar, in order to withstand abnormal abuse due to strenuous movement of the ship" pp. 7-8).

There are 35 single bricks in the collection and one cluster of four of whole bricks and fragments to which is attached an iron spike 13.8" (35 cm) long and 1.5" (4 cm) in diameter (Figure 13 a) The spike has a hex head about 2.4")6 cm) wide. The other bricks do not show traces of metal reinforcing. One brick (Figure 13 c) still has pieces of wood adhering to it and the others have varying amounts of mortar (Figure 13 b). The two illustrated bricks are a) 7.5 x 3.4 x 2.2" (19 x 8.5 x 5.5 cm) and b 7.9 x 3.5 x 2.4" (20x 9 x 6 cm). The remainder of the bricks is about the same size.

Double block, wood, iron, and brass (Figure 5 a): Although Pierce did not state where he found the object, it is probable that it is the cat block used to hoist the anchor. Such a block has an iron hook which attaches to the anchor and the entire unit is then attached by a tackle to the cat davit.

The piece in the collection consists of a wooden block with two wheels, bout securely in a rectangular iron frame. Inside the iron frame, two of the vertical wooden members remain; presumably there was a third which served as a spacer between the two wheels. The best preserved of the wooden piece is fitted tightly inside the metal frame. It seems likely that the metal was fitted while hot and thus shrank into place. The wooden piece is tapered at the end and wider in the middle.

Overall, the dimensions of the block are 7.9 x 11.8 (20 x 30 cm). The wooden side piece is about 3.2" (8 cm) wide at the ends, about 4.3" (.11 CM) at the middle, and about 1.2" (3 cm) thick. The metal frame is likewise tapered, about 1.6" (4 cm) wide at the base and about 2.4" (6 cm) at the top where there is a short segment of a fixed hook remaining.

The two wheels are each made from a single piece of wood, bored at the center and with brass flanges on either side which are fixed in place by means of screws. Inside the center perforation, there is a hexagonal-shaped socket, apparently made of iron. Since this shape would not permit the wheels to turn easily, one must suppose that a bushing or bearings are missing. The wheels turn on an iron axle, which is forged to the side members of the frame.

The wheels are 6.7: (17 cm) in diameter and 1,4" (3.5 cm) wide with grooves about, 3" (.75 cm) deep; thus, they would have held a rope of about 3/4 inch. Only about one-third of the perimeter of each wheel is presently grooved, lending some support to the idea that they did not turn during their last period of use.

The block was apparently dipped in hot was and perhaps sprayed by Dr. Pierce. In consequence, corrosion continued under the surface. The piece is thus in somewhat worse condition than when he recovered it. I have removed the rust scales; wire brushed the entire piece and melted most of the wax off. Following this treatment, I sprayed the iron portions with WD-40 to inhibit further rusting.[79]

This Crows Nest photo was taken by Steve Stepinoff, June 14, 1970. Picture taken from the dive team's rubber boat on their way to excavation.[80]

Steve Stepinoff recalled, "One time I pulled myself up into the crows nest, it was a crows nest, and observed that we were surrounded by clear cabbage jellyfish. Some of them stung us bad on our legs. Dr. Pierce had some Adolfo's meat tenderizer in his dive bag and we put it on our legs to soothe the stings. It helped a little, but it still hurt."

THE BOILER REMAINS OF THE STEAMSHIP, ACADIA,
A CONFEDERATE SIDEWHEELER, STAND ABOVE
THE WATERS OF THE GULF OF MEXICO.
THE ACADIA WAS A BLOCKADE RUNNER DURING THE CIVIL WAR
AND RAN AGROUND ON FEBRUARY 6, 1865 NEAR
VELASCO TX. THE SHIP WAS DESTROYED BY GUNFIRE
WHEN IT WAS DISCOVERED BY THE USS VIRIGINA

For over 100 years the Crows Nest of the *Acadia* stood above the water line in the Gulf of Mexico near San Luis Pass. Although the caption says she was a Confederate ship, which she was not, this is one of the few photos of the boiler stack and crows nest.[81]

Chapter Three
Divers that accompanied Dr. Wendell Pierce

Thirty plus years later, Mr. John R. Choate, Houston, Texas, Mr. Steve Stepinoff, Cypress, Texas and Mr. Mike Holt, Houston, Texas share their stories of diving with Dr. Pierce:

John R. Choate

Science teacher, skydiver, and a dive instructor worked with Dr. Wendell Pierce for about two years retrieving artifacts. Mr. Choate called Dr. Pierce "Magoo". Dr. Pierce would tie a telephone line to the axel of his Chrysler Imperial car, scuba gear on, with weights on his legs he would walk the sandy bottom and pull the line to the *Acadia*. The crew on shore would assist to retrieve the artifacts.

Mike James was the guy who roomed with one of my fellow diving instructors, Mike Holt. All I remember about James was that he was single, had a VW Bus and a three-legged dog.

John R. Choate of Pearland, Texas
Photo Courtesy John Choate

Holt and I were friends and roomed together during our 1971 NAUI Instructor's course, which we held at Rice University. I did not keep in touch with James for long after the day he first took me to the *Acadia* that first time. I have no idea where he is today nor can I find Mike Holt who sawed the screw off the shrimp boat adjacent to the Acadia. I do not think Steven Stepinoff knew James. I went on with my career as a NAUI Instructor with Scuba Inc. then as the register of The Ocean Corporation, which taught commercial diving. At the height of that career, I was appointed director of the 1974 NAUI Instructor's course, once again at Rice. I also received NAUI's Outstanding Contribution to Diving Award that year.

Attached is probably the only shot of me in Scuba gear I have. That was taken by my wife at Comal Park on Canyon Lake north of New Braunfels where we put our students in for the first of three dives, which were required in open water prior to certification. The sign in the background is a little ironic. That had to be prior to 1985.

— John Choate

Steve Stepinoff

Partner/President of Stepinoff-Crosier, a communication, branding and strategy firm working with Fortune 500 Corporations. I was a college student at the University of Houston and scuba instructor in my early years while diving with Dr. Wendell Pierce DDS on the CSS *Acadia*, a Confederate civil war blockade-runner, located on the Freeport side of San Luis Pass. Since Dr. Pierce had poor vision, I would drive him to the *Acadia* on the weekends and dive together with him and other friends to recover many artifacts over the span of about three years until his death on Sunday, October 7, 1973.

Dr. Pierce had a great love for archaeological underwater history and wanted to share his findings with future generations. I was so glad to be his friend and fellow diver to accomplish his goals.

Steve was one of the divers with Dr. Pierce. He also drove him from Houston to the wreck site and back. One day long before Steve met Dr. Pierce while on the beach, a woman ran up to Dr. Pierce asking if he could administer CPR to a drowning young man nearby. Rushing to store his gear and go help he accidentally put out his eye with the trunk lid of his car. Later that

Dive bell and Steve Stepinoff of Cypress, Texas. *Photo Courtesy of Steve Stepinoff*

day apparently, he noticed that he became blind in that eye. Dr. Pierce did perform CPR on the young man but he did not make it. Driving a car was no longer an option for Dr. Pierce. He lived in pain because of his eye injury from that day forward.

Steve explained that the Dr. Pierce letter is correct but he later replaced the inexpensive crab line 1/8 with a telephone line. He said it was much easier and stronger to hold on to while pulling ourselves to and from the *Acadia*.

We tied telephone wire to his car and sometimes to a water pipe we found on the beach to pull our raft and boat to the *Acadia*. Sometimes we just pulled ourselves to the *Acadia* by using the wire. It made is so much easier to get out to the wreck with was about 300 yards from the shoreline.

Regarding the Chemicals used to clean artifacts: he explained,

"Wendell called it his secret formula of Pluto-Pu: (I think he made up that name). He also mentioned cleaning the artifacts with muriatic acid, but he later added hydrochloric and sulfuric acids in each crockpot.!

We dipped each brass item into each crock pot for a few seconds then rinsed with water, then sprayed each artifact with Krylon Crystal Clear Spray Paint, gloss."

I was 18 when I met Dr. Pierce while I was working for Scuba Inc. Which was purchased by Oceaneering and the new division was renamed, The Ocean Corporation. John Choate also worked there. We were both Diving instructors there too. John taught with the commercial divers and I worked on the retail side and sometimes helped on the commercial side while I went to the University of Houston. I worked and studied there while I was in school.

Wendell came in one day to get his tank filled and that is how I met him. He asked me if I would like to accompany him on diving and recovering artifacts from the *Acadia*. I thought that would be so cool! And it was indeed.

Steve Stepinoff

A Story about
Dr. Pierce Raft Drifting to Sea by Steve Stepinoff

I used to drive Wendell down to the *Acadia* almost every weekend and leave my car at his house. He could not see well enough to drive. One weekend, we had the new homemade "boat" we in tow. We launched it to take out to the Acadia on Saturday. Tied it up to the mast and proceeded to recover artifacts and place them in the box on the bow of our "boat". We spent the night on the beach and continued diving until about 4:00 pm when I told Wendell that I had to go to school so I needed to head back to Houston. He told me to take his car home to his house and he would continue diving on the *Acadia*. I swam back to the shore and drove back to his house and told Eva to go back on Monday to pick him up at the *Acadia*.

About a couple days later I received a call from Wendell and he told me that he got tired and untied the boat. so he could drift back to the shore. Well, the current had apparently taken him out to sea instead of to the shore. He said he was so tired he fell asleep while the boat drifted out to sea. As a note, the boat had a 10-foot wooden mast with a confederate flag on it. Apparently, another boat, he said the Coast Guard, spotted the flag and approached it where they found Wendell laying on the top of the boat and rescued him back to shore. That is the story he gave me. Knowing Wendell, it was the truth. This kind of thing could only happen to him several miles offshore. I would imagine his wife Eva was freaked-out about the whole incident!

Then he asked me if we were going back out there the following weekend. I told him that I had a sore throat and may not be able to go. He told me to come to his dentist office so he could look at it. So, I met him up there after school that evening, as I remember. While he was looking in my mouth his wife, Eva, unannounced to me, gave me a Penicillin shot in the arm while at the same exact time, Wendell took some forceps with cotton drenched in a red chemical and shoved it down my throat. Coating my throat in this awful stuff. I passed out the dentist chair! When I came to, Wendell said I should be well by Saturday to go back to the *Acadia*. Well, he was right and we went back out there the following weekend. He was relentless!

I remember while diving on the *Acadia* that one of the paddle wheels was intact and the other one was laying over on its side."

Steve Stepinoff

Deputy Sheriff (Lee) D. H. Page of the Brazoria County Sheriff's Office.

Steve Stepinoff shared a scary story about him and Dr. Pierce while walking along the beach back to Dr. Pierce's car one afternoon. "A car with two men in it stopped and offered them a ride. With artifacts in hand, they declined. Then the deputy showed up and they told him the story. He said, oh my goodness, good thing you did not accept! We are looking for them, they are mass murders." The murderer was Henry Lee Lucas and his accomplice."[83]

I had thought to mention, this may sound strange but . . . I was remembering back in the 70's while diving on the *Acadia* . . . When I was pulling myself out to the *Acadia* on the telephone line that Wendell and I tied to the mast of the ship and to the shore, as I got closer to the ship, while

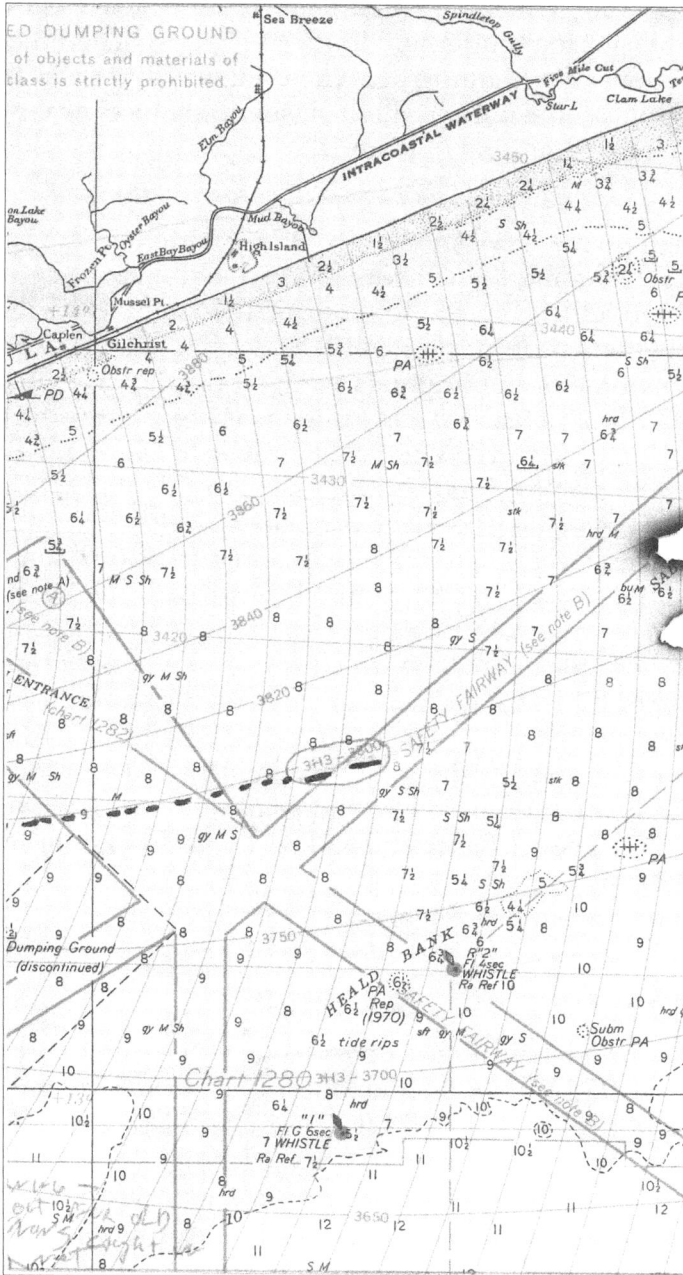

Map found in Dr. Pierce papers, Brazoria County Historical Museum may be where the U.S. Coast Guard found him in the raft. Steve Stepinoff says he was about that far out in the Gulf of Mexico.[82]

underwater with full scuba gear, I could hear "clicking" sounds getting louder and louder as I approached the *Acadia*. I never could figure out what that was, but I was thinking it was some kind of shellfish snapping its claws together to make that kind of sound???

The El Matanceros

I dove the *El Matanceros* in 1975. Wendell told me about it prior to going there. I was 18-years-old then.

Wendell and I used to replicate the "double" crucifixes in his dentist office on Fannin Street. He made dozens of them. Some of the originals were on display in the Museum of Natural Science. Dr. Pulley was the curator then and was a great friend to Wendell and myself. I wish I was able to have one then but they were made of dental gold and I would never ask Dr. Pierce for one.

Several years later, my wife and I took our son, who was five at the time, to Akumal, Mexico, at the beach site where we dove the *El Matanceros* to show him the cannons that were placed on the beach facing the wreck. I have a photo of him sitting on one of them on the shoreline.

As a sidebar, I used to go to Mexico, Monterrey, and Guadalajara, on business quite regularly and worked with Pablo Bush's son in law in the printing business together. We were good friends and talked about his father-in-law and diving quite a bit.

Fun days indeed! It is not so safe anymore.

Steve Stepinoff

Mike Holt

I started teaching scuba at the YMCA in Vancouver, B.C. in 1964. Came to Houston in 1966. In 1969 I started to teach at the DADS CLUB YMCA. In 1972 I became a NAUI Instructor. In 2006 I retired. from teaching.

I met Dr. McGoo in the late 60's or early 70's on the beach near the *Acadia*. He was running more line to the wreck and we help him with that. That part of the beach has a number sandbars so you can walk over the bars and each time the water gets deeper till you are up to your neck and a few hundred feet from the wreck. You are approx.

1000 feet from the beach. At that point, you have to swim. The water has *NO* visibility most of the time on a good day you can see a few inches

The wreck *Acadia* is far enough off the beach that shrimpers could get their nets tangled in the wreck this made for a very spooky and potentially dangerous dive.

On one trip out there, I tripped over what turned out to be an old shrimp boat. On a later dive, we discovered that the prop was still there. All we had to do was saw through the 3-inch brass shaft and pull it back it to the beach. What a find. Not that easy.

A few weeks later I took my advanced diver class to the aquarium in Galveston for a fish I.D. class and then we would do SURF entries in Galveston You guessed it; the gulf was dead flat, no surf.

I sent the class home and a couple of us went to the *Acadia*. We were able to saw through the shaft in approximately twenty minutes due to the fact we had no waves. The next day we went back with lots of rope and a lift bag and pulled the anchor to the beach.

Back then the historical plaque on the road was east of the wreck and I don't know if they ever moved it before the "crow's nest fell over.

Mike Holt

The collection itself now resides at the Brazoria County Historical Museum in Angleton, Texas, where its materials are often featured in exhibitions and are available for study by researchers. *Photo Courtesy of Steve Stepinoff*

Article from *The Facts* Jan 14, 2018

ANGLETON — Texas never saw near the ground activity as other states during the Civil War, but action in the coastal waters were plentiful.

Ships loaded with military supplies, civilian goods and commodities to be sold overseas would depart from Texas ports routinely, attempting to get past the Union blockade.

In honor of National Archaeology Month, the Brazoria County Historical Museum is holding an exhibition of items salvaged from the wreck of the county's best-known blockade-runner, the *Acadia*, throughout the month of October.

"The old-timers referred to it as 'the boilers' because they stuck up above the water for a long, long time," museum curator Mike Bailey said.

According to the *Handbook of Texas Online,* the side-wheel steamer was on its first voyage as a blockade-runner when it ran aground on a sandbar on Feb. 6, 1865, near San Luis Pass, 10 miles from its destination at the mouth of the Brazos River.

Shore parties from Galveston immediately salvaged most of the ship's cargo, but when the fog cleared that day, the Union ship USS *Virginia* spotted the *Acadia* and opened fire, destroying it.

The ship's cargo of some military — but mostly civilian — goods, including cloth, hand tools, and canned fruit, was salvaged immediately by shore parties and sold at auction in Galveston.

The museum's collection of about 300 items salvaged from the *Acadia* in the 1970s mostly are parts of the actual ship. They include door knobs, hinges, locks, keys and the like, Bailey said,

There are, however, a few other objects that were taken from the ship and will be on display, such as ceramic jugs and the unlikely centerpiece of the collection, an early flush toilet, he said.

"Our first thought was that it was an early Crapper, but it turned out it's not," Bailey said, referring to John Crapper, one of the flush toilet's earliest marketers.

Strangely enough, that object has a broad appeal among

This photo was taken in the kitchen of Dr. Pierce. Today the artifacts are numbered and are housed at the Brazoria County Historical Museum.[84]

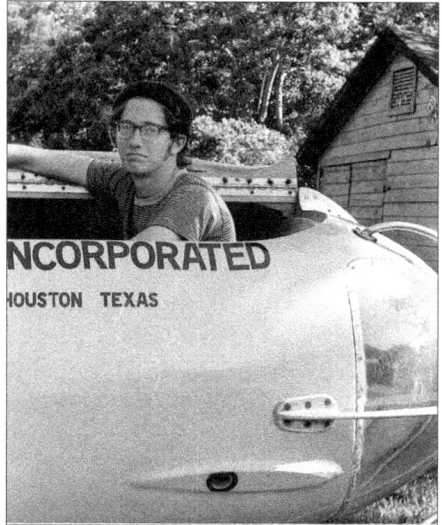

A 1970s photo of Steve Stepinoff in the the wet-submarine that was used to tow behind a boat for observation of pipelines, etc.

Michael Bailey, Curator at the Brazoria County Historical Museum, shows off an old toilet now on display as part of a Civil War shipwreck exhibit.

museum visitors.

"That's one of our best artifacts," Information Services Coordinator Jamie Murray said. "Everyone is enchanted with the toilet."

Acadia items aren't on display very often, she said, "so it's about time."

It is actually interesting that a man's name, Thomas E. Crapper, can be not only a be a Noun but also a Verb!

Thomas Crapper called his invention the Crapper's Valveless Water Waste Preventer (Patent #4,9900). There is a book in the Rice University library called *Flushed with Pride*, by Thomas Crapper.

Memo regarding The Facts Article

I remember diving with Dr. Pierce when we salvaged the "crapper". Actually, we pulled up two crappers that same day. There were two separate crates encrusted with encrustations and silt. Officer Page with the Brazoria County Sheriff's Department assisted us by blocking the drive-by traffic while we managed to pull the crates out of the water and onto the shore.

Steve Stepinoff—regard article in the *Fact* Jan 14, 2018

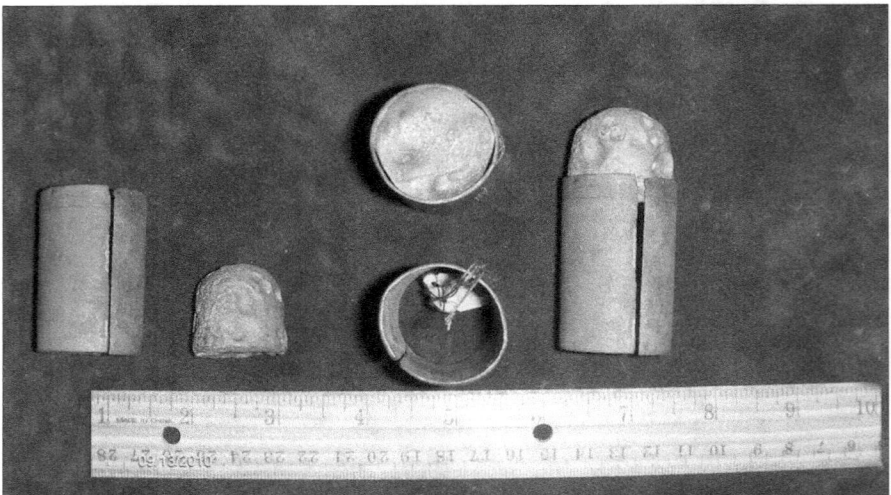

Recovered ammunition from *Acadia*; possibly used for Williams Smoothbore Repeating Gun manufactured by Williams Gun in Richmond, Virginia. Only forty were made.

Two-gallon stoneware jug recovered by Dr. Wendell E. Pierce from the *Acadia*.

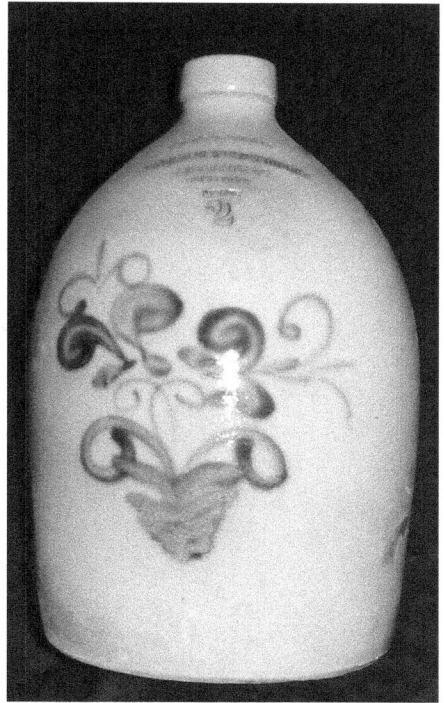

News Article Quebec
Translation
E &W Poston Cie, Importer
They advertise a sale on the Lower Québec city (lower town market For tea tobacco oil coffee spices and liquor and that they have a large assortment and very low price for a business manager.

Second paragraph—— It is an ad for dealers and the ad says that they have on a large quantity of wine and liquor and that they will have a great price on the lower town market Québec city on the 9 of October 1857

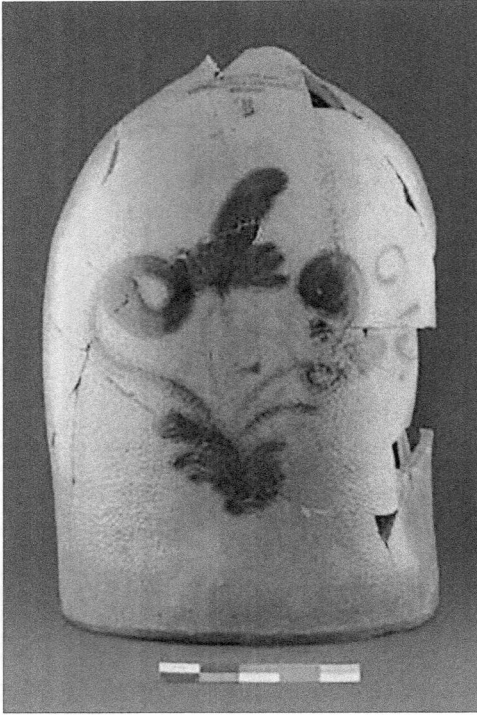

Quebec Jug

Response from Quebec Art Museum:

We don't know for sure where in North America this jar was made, but there is an inscription on it: "E. & W. POSTON & Co / WINE & SPIRIT MERCHANTS / QUEBEC / 3".

This jar was found in Place Royale, in the oldest part of Quebec City.

Regards,

Andréane Beloin
Conseillère en patrimoine

Direction générale du patrimoine
Ministère de la Culture et des Communications
225, Grande Allée Est, bloc C, R.-C.
Québec (Québec) G1R 5G5

Téléphone : 418 380-2352

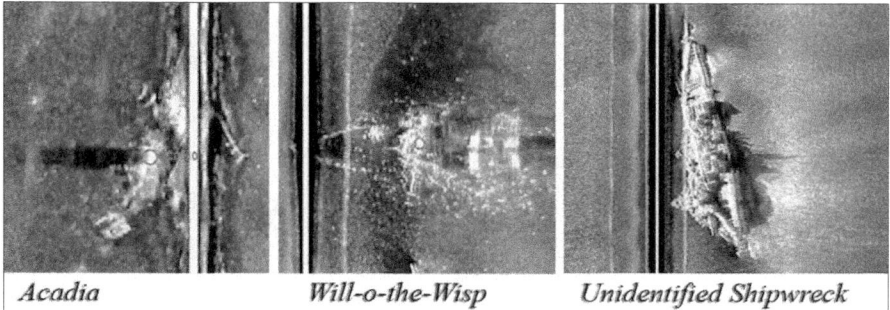

| *Acadia* | *Will-o-the-Wisp* | *Unidentified Shipwreck* |

Sunken Blockade Runners off Texas Coast. *Photo Courtesy of Texas General Land Office*[86]

Wendell E. Pierce D.D.S.
3817 Fannin St.
Suite No. 4
Houston, Texas 77004

October 18, 1970

Re: Texas State Historical Marker

Mr. Truett Lattimer, Executive Director
Texas State Historical Survey Commission
PO Box 12276
Capitol Station
Austin, Texas

Dear Sir:

Through the encouragement and interest of Dr. T. Pulley, Director of the "Houston Museum of Natural Science", I have pursued the accurate historical facts of the so-called boilers that a monument has been erected to by the Texas State Historical Committee, as reference of the above mentioned. (copy enclosed). The information that presently exists upon this marker is in contrast to the results of my research.

In my report, which is enclosed, you will note that several artifacts have been recovered and treated for presentation and display and are now in my possession. Naturally, it would please me for these artifacts to be displayed in the "Houston Museum of Natural Science" along with the historical information. However, I thoroughly understand that this decision is the responsibility of your committee.

You can indeed expect my complete cooperation in this matter to the best of my ability.

Sincerely,
Wendell E. Pierce, D.D.S.

A display of *Acadia* artifacts made by Dr. Pierce with the Confederate flag. *Photo courtesy of Steve Stepinoff*

For so many years it was thought the *Acadia* was a Confederate owned blockage runner. Not so, she was a British owned blockage runner with a crew that tried to deliver goods to the Confederate military forts near San Luis Pass, Texas.

There are many sunken Civil War ships in the Gulf of Mexico.

The *Acadia* remains where she ran aground. Although she is out of sight, she remains historically as one of the best fishing spots on the Texas coast.

End Notes

Part One

1. Wikipedia: Flags and flag etiquette. In Fowler, Jean (Ed.): Reed's Nautical Almanac 1992, pp. 13:1–13:8. East Molesey: Thomas Reed Publications. ISBN 0-947637-96-6 Public Domain

2. President Lincoln's Order to Secretary of State to create a blockade of Southern Ports Image Courtesy of the Raab Collection, Ardmore, PA

3. Public Domain President Abraham Lincoln

4. *Clyde Built Blockade Runners Cruisers and Armored Rams of the American Civil War* by Eric J. Graham.

5. The Ports of Halifax and Saint John and the American Civil War Greg Marquis "Running the Blockade"

6. Lincennes misspelled.

7. Dr. Frank Hole, Department of Anthropology and Archeology, Rice University, is to write the official publication for the Archives of the State of Texas, and shall serve as the legal adoption papers of another heroine of Texas History.

8. National Park Service Department of the Interior "The American Civil War."

9. National Park Service.

10. THE BLOCKADE RUNNERS FROM "The Navy in the Civil War, Vol. 1 James Russell Soley, USN https://www.battlefields.org/learn/articles/how-cite-american-battlefield-trust

11. City of Texas City – Museum, Texas City, Texas phonograph Boiler USS Westfield.

12. Sorel-Tracy Wikipedia.

13. https://en.wikipedia.org/wiki/Sorel-Tracy.

14. *une photo prise en* 1979 *du batiment historique* Sincennes-McNaughton Line. I *Gracieusete* ,

15. *Pour des idées d'activités dans la région de* Sorel-Tracy, *suivez-nous sur* Facebook! *Devez-vous imprimer ce courriel? Si oui, pensez l'imprimer recto-verso!*

16. Frederick H. Armstrong, "SINCENNES, JACQUES-FÉLIX," in *Dictionary of Canadian Biography*, vol. 10, University of Toronto/Université Laval, 2003–, accessed August 2, 2017, http://www.biographi.ca/en/bio/sincennes_jacques_felix_10E.html. http://www.biographi.ca/en/bio/sincennes_jacques_felix_10E.html Author of Article: Frederick H. Armstrong Title of Article: SINCENNES, JACQUES-FÉLIXDictionary of Canadian Biography, vol. 10 University of Toronto/Université Laval 1972, August 2, 2018

17. "OCLC Leadership" www.oclc.org ©2018 OCLC Online Computer Library Center 19 January 2018

18. ST LAWRENCE SAGA: THE CLARKE STEAMSHIP STORY Kevin Griffin Chapter 2

19. *Outaouais' Forest History* - Canals, tug-boats and barges http://www.histoireforestiereoutaouais.ca/en/c23/#9 19 No image : 3727378

20. *Les Bateaux de la Cie Sincenne Mc Noughton dans le port de Sorel, P.Q.by Thos. Jefferys Cote* : BAnQ, CP 021375 CON

21. 'I © Illustrated London News Ltd/Mary Evans. Image created courtesy of THE BRITISH LIBRARY BOARD. Image reproduced with kind permission of The British Newspaper Archive (www.britishnewspaperarchive.co.uk)'

22. Pressreader *Ross's Weekly* April 28, 2018

23.*Halifax Sun and Advertizer*, Fri, Aug 26, 1864 Newspaperarchive May 1, 2018.

24. *Halifax Citizen* Halifax, Nova Scotia Sat Aug. 27, 1864 Page 2.

26. *Ibid.*

27. *Halifax Sun* November 7, 1864 Sunday M O'B - from Greg Marquis.

28. *Official records of the Union and Confederate Navies in the War of the Rebellion*; Series I - Volume 3: The Operation of the Cruisers (April 1, 1864 - December 30, 1865).

29. *Daily Alta California,* Volume 21, Number 6944, 23 March 1869

30. *Ibid.*

31. Public Archives of Canada Record Group 42, Volume 117. No 154

32. Newspaper Archives *Halifax Citizen* Halifax, Nova Scotia 4/18/18 https://newspaperarchive.com/ca/nova-scotia/halifax/halifax-citizen4

33. *Daily Alta California*, Volume 21, Number 6944, 23 March 1869

34. *Ibid.*

35. *Ibid.*

36. *Clarke County Times Enterprise* Mississippi Dec. 14, 1905

37. Map of the Atlantic Seaboard, Gulf of Mexico and West Indies. Phantom of Anglo-Confederate Commerce: An Historical and Archaeological Investigation of American Civil War Blockade Running. Gordon P Watts. A Thesis Submitted for the Degree of PhD at the University of St Andrews, 1997 http://hdl.handle.net/10023/2891 6/4/18

38. January 1, 1865, Page 3 The New York Times Archives, https://newspaperarchive.com/ca/nova-scotia/halifax/halifax-citizen4/18/18

39. *Halifax Citizen* December 6, 1864 4/28/18.

40. *Royal Gazette Bermuda Commercial and General Advertiser and Recorder*, Dec. 13, 1864

41. *Bermuda Royal Gazette*. Hamilton, December 20, 1864-April 25, 2018 http://bnl.contentdm.oclc.org/cdm/ref/collection/BermudaNP02/id/12112.

42. *New York Times* December 24, 1864.

43. *Buffalo Morning Express* and *Illustrated Buffalo Express*, Buffalo New York, 30 Dec 1864 Page 2

44. *Hartford Courant*, Hartford Connecticut 30 Dec 1864 Page 2.

45. *Madison Courier*, Madison, Indiana Feb. 8, 1865 Newspaper archives.

46. *Galveston Weekly News*, Feb. 15, 1865.

47. *Cleveland Leader* E Cowles & Co, daily Two Editions Morning and Evening Vol XIX. No 53 March 1, 1865.

48. *Royal Gazettte Bermuda Commercial and General Advertiser and Recorder* Vol XXXVIII March 14, 1865.

49. by W. Jowrick Galveston-Tri-Weekly February 21, 1865

50. The following, adapted from the *Chicago Manual of Style*, 15th edition, is the preferred citation for this article. *Handbook of Texas Online*, Matthew K. Hamilton, "Fifth Texas Infantry," accessed November 02, 2017, http://www.tshaonline.org/handbook/online/articles/qkf11.

51. Richard M. Venable Capt. & Chief of Topographical Engineers, West Louisianan and Arkansas (District), Dec 24th, 1864, delivered in person to the Bureau, by Lt Col H T Douglas, Corp of Engineers

52. *Ibid.*

53, Naval History and Heritage Command 12/20/17 permission.

54. Dr. Wendell Pierce collection.

55. Courtesy *Brazosport Facts*, March 13, 1966.

56. John H. Sterrett Born in Pennsylvania (1815–18 June 1879) was a ship captain or master of fourteen ships and investor of Houston and Galveston Navigation Company.

57. *Pleasant Paces* by Anne Ayers Lide McCurdy.

58.Brazoria County Historical Museum.

59. *Houston Tri-Weekly Telegraph*, February 10, 1965 (courtesy of Andrew W. Hall).

60. Brazoria County Historical Museum.

61. *Galveston Weekly* February 22, 1865.

62. Brazoria County Historical Museum.

63. Courtesy of Rosenberg Library

64. C. Patrick Labadie Collection / Thunder Bay National Marine Sanctuary, Alpena, MI. April 20, 2018

65. Hamiliton Public Library

66. *Voici deux* photos *originales de cet incendie historique du mois de Mai* 2016.

Part Two

67. Photo gift from Steve Stepinoff.

68. Sunday March 21, 1971 *Houston Chronicle*.

69. *LocoGringo*, Published by KayWalten.

70. *Ibid.*

71. Website search results for https://vimeo.com/3993300.

72. *Mexican Caribbean*: By Earl J. Wilson.

73. Acadia Binder, Steve Stepinoff.

74. Letter from Dr. Wendell Pierce Research Files, Brazoria County Historical Museum- Accession Number 2013.024c.0002.

75. *The Facts*, June 30, 1976.

76. Antiquities Committee Truett Lattimer, Chairman or Executive Secretary, Dr. T.C. Pulley, Director of the Houston Museum of Natural Science, Dr Frank Hole, Department of Anthropology and Archeology, Rice University.

77. The Acadia Notes by Frank Hole. pages have been transcribed by the author.

78. Steve Stepinoff, 4/4/18.

79. Hole, Frank. "The Acadia: A Civil War Blockade Runner," Technical Report Number One. Department of Anthropology. Houston, TX: Rice University, 1974. Brazoria County Historical Museum.

80. Crows Nest —Dr Wendell Pierce files, Brazoria County Historical Museum.

81. Brazoria County Historical Museum BCHM Accession Number 2006.017p.0001.

Part Three

82. Brazoria County Historical Museum Dr. Wendell Pierce collection.

83. Henry Lee Lucas from Biography.com.

84. Dr Wendell Pierce Collection Brazoria County Historical Museum.

85. Brazoria County Historical Museum HPIM2656.JPEG.

86. Texas General Land Office Photo.

87. Display photo with Confederate Flag, gifted from Steve Stepinoff.

Index

About the Author

Eileen M Benitz Wagner has devoted her business career to product design, manufacturing, and national sales for the wholesale floral, nursery and mass merchant markets throughout the United States. As an owner of a small business, each category demands unlimited attention.

The late 1990s took her to the agricultural field and the growing of newly planted wine grapes. During this period she traveled to the wine grape regions of France, Canada, Chile, Argentina and Australia seeking additional information to improve her product.

A founding member of the International Pirates, (a charity entertainment group from across America) that began in the middle 1980s, she sang and danced to warm the hearts of elderly, special needs children, Shrine Burn Hospital patients and all she met as a Lady Pirate. "It is giving something back. We say it is putting a little color in black and white worlds when nothing but pain is in sight."

Her love of history and having lived at Treasure Island, San Luis Pass, Texas, since 1981 became her passion to save this portion of Texas history which has never been written about. She was awarded the 2019 Dan Parkinson Literary Award which the Old Fort Velasco Historical Association and the Old Velasco/Surfside Beach Historical Committee award each year to an individual who has used his/her writing ability to promote the rich history of Brazoria County.

She lives in The Woodlands, Texas, near her family. One daughter lives in Dallas and the other lives in Spring, Texas.

Additional Works by the Author

Senator Max E. Benitz, Sr.: "Mr. Energy"
By Eileen M. Benitz Wagner & Michelle Gerber Ph.D

The Ghost City of San Luis Island
By Eileen M. Benitz Wagner

www.ingramcontent.com/pod-product-compliance
Lightning Source LLC
LaVergne TN
LVHW051351080426
835509LV00020BA/3389